Naked
Intimacy

Naked Intimacy

How to Increase
True Openness in Your
Relationship

Joel D. Block, Ph.D.

Contemporary Books

Chicago   New York   San Francisco   Lisbon   London   Madrid   Mexico City
Milan   New Delhi   San Juan   Seoul   Singapore   Sydney   Toronto

The **McGraw·Hill** Companies

Library of Congress Cataloging-in-Publication Data

Block, Joel D.
    Naked intimacy : how to increase true openness in your relationship / Joel D. Block.
        p.   cm.
    Includes bibliographical references and index.
    ISBN 0-07-139518-0 (acid-free paper)
      1. Marriage.   2. Communication in marriage.   3. Honesty.
   4. Intimacy (Psychology)   I. Title

   HQ734.B656   2002
   646.7'8—dc21   2002023448

2 3 4 5 6 7 8 9 0   DOC/DOC   1 0 9 8 7 6

ISBN 0-07-139518-0

Cover photo copyright © Robert Llewellyn/SuperStock

McGraw-Hill books are available at special quantity discounts to use as premiums and sales promotions, or for use in corporate training programs. For more information, please write to the Director of Special Sales, Professional Publishing, McGraw-Hill, Two Penn Plaza, New York, NY 10121-2298. Or contact your local bookstore.

This book is printed on acid-free paper.

To Gail,

for who you are and what we share

CONTENTS

AUTHOR'S NOTE

The identities of the people described in this book were protected by altering names and other external characteristics, but the basic psychological and social dynamics involved have been preserved. Any resemblance to real persons is strictly intended; any precise identification with real persons is, I trust, impossible.

Some of the terms used throughout the book require clarification. The terms *wife, husband, spouse, love partner, relationship,* and *marriage,* are used interchangeably with the intention of including all couples, married or not. In no instance are these terms meant to exclude anyone. For the issues of emotional openness that I address are fundamental. All couples face them. I have thought it best to give examples only on the basis of my own professional experience, which has been primarily with male-female couples. Yet it is my hope that this book will prove helpful to any two people engaged in an ongoing love relationship of any type.

INTRODUCTION

HOW THIS BOOK WAS BORN

Opening our heart is a requirement in a love relationship. It is not optional. If we are afraid of revealing ourselves, love may never develop, or it may wither quietly. Whether love that isn't nurtured by authenticity never blossoms or simply deteriorates over time is not important. In either case, it will ultimately be unsatisfactory.

A few months ago, my wife, Gail, and I were having lunch when Karen, a casual friend whom we see once in a great while, came in and greeted us. She was alone, and when Gail asked her to join us she smiled receptively and sat down. "What's new?" I asked. "How's Ron doing?" Karen looked at me and then turned to Gail. "We're getting divorced," she announced. We were surprised and puzzled.

Karen and Ron seemed to be in good spirits with each other at the occasional social gatherings we attended that bring couples together. Karen was an office manager, an outgoing sort of person. Ron was a research scientist at a local hospital. Though neither Gail nor I knew them in any personal way, Karen seemed like she wouldn't be a difficult person to get along with; Ron seemed amicable as well. So, what happened? While I was thinking about whether to ask, Gail turned to her and posed the question.

Karen seemed eager to talk. They didn't fight much, she said; neither was having an affair. But she felt disconnected from Ron. She said they never talked about anything except domestic problems. The garage needed to be cleaned up again; their son, Billy, needed to be driven to a friend's house; the bedroom needed a coat of paint. She knew that I was a psychologist specializing in working with couples and that Gail was a social worker. Her decision didn't make sense to most people, even those in her family, and she hoped we didn't think she had simply gone off the deep end.

In a way, she said, it would have been easier if Ron had been sneaking off to bed with one of his colleagues at the hospital or if he had been abusive. But it was simply that after almost twenty years they had nothing to say to each other. The only real connection between them was the children, and now the children were adolescents and would soon be gone. They had simply grown apart, she said. It was as if they were strangers who shared a history and a roof. That was not what she wanted. She wanted to make a change before it was too late.

Karen's feelings had crystallized one day while she was at the anniversary celebration of a friend. Some of the couples there also seemed to be living together separately, but there were a few who seemed to be in love. They looked at each other with interest, and when they spoke it wasn't just small talk; it was personal and intimate. She hungered for that and wanted it in her life. She wanted it badly enough to break up her family, to put her husband and her children through the inevitable trauma and acrimony of divorce.

Was she wrong to be doing this? She didn't actually ask the question, but it was written all over her. She said she thought about the consequences all the time. At first, Ron agreed to go for any kind of help she wanted. After a brief trial of marriage counseling with two different therapists, Karen decided it was useless. He infuriated her, even though he was intelligent, thoughtful, and a successful scientist.

While Ron could speak brilliantly about science, when it came to his feelings, even for Karen, he was at a loss. Try as she might to elicit an emotional response from him, her efforts resulted only in mutual frustration. "I don't naturally express my feelings," he told the therapist they had seen at Karen's insistence. Ron was a decent guy, Karen said, but he was so closed, she felt lonely with him. "He didn't even make eye contact with the therapist as he spoke," Karen complained. The loneliness she felt was more painful than being alone. She didn't want to live with him and build more resentment toward him.

Leaving Ron came with a steep price. The divorce process began cooperatively, but that didn't last long. After Ron moved out, their daughter dyed her hair purple, had her nose pierced, and began to skip school. Their son, the younger of the two, would call Ron late at night and beg to come over. Shortly after he got there, without explanation, he would want to go back home. He was by turns moody, nervous, clingy, and short-tempered. Both kids blamed Karen for the split and gave her a hard time. One day her son said with fury and tears, "How could you do this to Dad?!" Karen nearly broke down in the face of his anguish.

On the drive home Gail and I were locked in an intense discussion of what had happened with Karen. The couples that come to me for help with their relationship don't usually declare that their partners are decent but just don't have much to say. They complain of their inability to resolve disagreements, of feeling unappreciated, of being criticized and judged. Consider, for example, a couple having their first meeting with me. A psychologist I was training in couple therapy was observing them. Their interactions were colorful and intense; each blamed the other for the unhappiness and confronted the other with "the truth." The psychologist-in-training told me afterward that she was impressed that "real feelings" were being expressed.

From my perspective, however, there was little exchange of real feelings between the husband and wife, although I don't doubt the presence of real pain. The contagious reactivity between them was so high that almost any topic triggered a reflexive and intensive counter that threw them into rigidly polarized camps. Neither could identify the issues that really caused their pain, hear the other objectively, or take a position without blaming or telling the other what to do. Their exchanges were about accusations and counteraccusations, not about the hurt and sadness hiding behind the anger.

After a while these couples start feeling as if they are walking across a verbal minefield with each other. One wrong word can set off an explosion. They are so sensitized to each other that a slight change of facial expression or tone of voice, barely discernible to the uninitiated, can set off a storm of accusations that escalates until one or the other gives up in utter frustration and despair. In fact, the week following our lunch with Karen we were witness to just this sort of demonstration.

We were waiting in a line that circled around the interior of a popular bakery on a Sunday morning. A man who looked to be in his late thirties stalked out the door a moment after we had entered, his face set in an expression both stony and sullen, with a stiff body posture that suggested contained rage. Just before he stormed off he had complained to his partner that the line was moving too slowly and he feared he would be late for his pickup basketball game. She looked at him blankly without saying anything. "What, you have a problem with me taking time for myself?" he snapped.

Close on his heels his partner jumped out of the line and ran after him, her fists desperately pummeling his back while she yelled, "Goddamn you! Tell me what you're feeling!"

"I'm not feeling anything," he insisted.

"Who can feel nothing?" she cried.

"I can!" he screamed.

"Get back here," she screamed back. "Talk to me, yell, cry, do something, you bastard!"

That poignant, desperate plea aimed at a retreating back epitomizes a pattern seen in couples: she seeks to engage but out of frustration does so in just the way that will hasten his retreat. And the more she presses, the more likely he will accelerate his withdrawal. He feels unsafe with her outbursts, and she feels his distant behavior has made her into a shrieking shrew.

Before long, the only topics remaining are those that are safe—talk about the kids and gossip about other people. Given some time, even these subjects wear thin, and then there is the "We have nothing in common" complaint. Is that what happened to Karen's marriage?

What Karen wanted was to recapture the excitement of the early part of her relationship, the time of discovery and openness. What's more, she apparently felt strong enough about it to take a dramatic stand. Many people in relationships feel as she does: lonely, occasionally casting a furtive glance at the person with whom they have been sharing a home for many years and wondering who that person really is. Some settle for their stable but unsatisfactory arrangement. Many others, as the staggeringly high divorce rates attest, opt out. Distressed marriages take two forms, with endless variations—either fight or flight; neither is satisfying, and neither fulfills the promise of what real openness and honesty can bring to a love relationship.

It is ironic that people who are sharing their lives are often less open with each other than they are with other people who are not as important to their lives. And therein lies the rub. It is because a person is important in our life that we become guarded. Their view of us matters more; they are central to our lives, and we want their validation. We want them to see things our way, especially those things that are dear to us. If one is excited by a movie, he or she wants the other to be excited as well. If one has a difficult experience and is upset and the other is not, that may cause a problem; one or both feel the other is reacting improperly. If one feels like sex and the other doesn't, there is resentment.

The relationship starts to resemble the interaction we had with our parents as children; it is about getting our love partner's approval and avoiding negative judgment. The feelings of rejection and sensitivity are unequaled in any other relationship.

"It's amazing," Gail said. "You would think that people who are unhappy with each other wouldn't get hung up on this validation stuff any longer. They just wouldn't care, and they would let it all hang out. In a weird way they can finally be themselves because there is so little at stake."

"Not being happy with each other doesn't diminish the desire for approval," I said. "It increases it. Look at what happens to people in a divorce battle—they are ready to fight to the death over every word, and they hate each other."

Gail looked at me thoughtfully. "You know," she said, "this is really something that no one talks about, the nature of true intimacy—being open, emotionally naked—in a committed relationship. Isn't that what we all want, to be able to be truly ourselves and be accepted? We camouflage our true being to protect ourselves. Intimacy is scary, because when you permit yourself to be known, when you really reveal yourself, you expose yourself not only to deep loving, but also to deep hurt."

Gail was talking to someone—her husband—who leads a double life. Not the kind that would make a good movie. The double life is as a psychologist and a writer. As we continued discussing the issues underlying Karen's decision to leave Ron, an idea was forming. It wasn't long before Gail noticed the look. We've been married a long time, and she has seen it often.

"You're going to write about this, aren't you?" she challenged.

"I would love to do a book about openness in relationships," I confessed. "A lot of the fighting and bickering between couples is because they have lost the kind of honest soul-baring intimacy that they had during their courtship. Most of their squabbles are really substitutes for the real thing; I'm talking about authentic openness between two people in a love relationship, the kind that is too rare. I would like to dig into what it is, what stands in the way, how to foster it and maintain it. I'm talking about being able to stand naked, figuratively, in front of your love partner. Taking off your clothes is easy, but what about disrobing emotionally? That's a different, more complex, and ultimately more satisfying experience. After all, if you can establish that kind of emotional closeness, there is nothing to sweat in the small stuff, because the rest really is just that, small stuff."

"Real openness between love partners is a controversial subject," Gail said. "It can be argued, for example, that not everyone wants that kind of intimacy. Indeed, the popular media strongly suggest that men are overwhelmed by the need of many women for more self-disclosure."

"That may be true, but why are so many men depressed, why are so many people dying prematurely, and how come divorce is epidemic?" I countered. "The status quo is certainly not thriving. Maybe there is a connection. . . ."

Is there a limit to openness; can it go too far and be detrimental? Don't people in relationships have a right to privacy? Can openness exist in an atmosphere that is not always supportive? What about secrecy—are there some things that should never be shared? How do we know if we are being reasonably cautious, or fearful of intimacy? What role does our upbringing have on the degree of openness we seek in our adult love relationships? Is there a way around defensiveness, especially the kind that is protective of very sensitive issues? These are some of the questions that we threw back and forth that afternoon.

And that's how the book began. It had been something I had been thinking about in relation to the couples I've worked with in therapy and in relation to myself in my own marriage. After the lunch with Karen, I was moved to talk to more couples about their experiences and put their thoughts together with mine. The book that grew out of this centers on the experience we all long for from the beginning of our lives—to be regarded and accepted as the person we truly are. We want that experience in childhood, and it is often thwarted by the need for our parents' approval. We lose a part of ourselves in our effort to fit their vision of us.

Marriage provides us with another opportunity to discover and nurture our true selves. When it works, that is love at its best. Often, however, marriage becomes something other than an opportunity to discover and foster our true selves. It becomes a war zone where real feeling and true openness are replaced by deception, defensiveness, and alienation. The goal of this book is to put marriage back where it belongs—on the high road—by providing an understanding of what naked intimacy really is and offering user-friendly suggestions on how to get it.

For one human being to love another, that is perhaps the most difficult of all our tasks, the ultimate, the last test and proof, the work for which all other work is but preparation.

—RAINER MARIA RILKE

I

THE MANY FACES OF
DECEPTION

*What about those everyday deceptions? Do they really matter? They
are typically viewed as harmless. In truth, they are like psychological termites, each bite barely perceptible until the very foundation
of love weakens. And, like termites attacking a home, once the
foundation of a relationship weakens, it requires a monumental
effort to rebuild.*

The beginning of love is wonderful. It is the subject of songs and the
theme of movies; it has created an industry in fiction writing, the
romance novel. But the test of love comes over time, the time beyond
the courtship and honeymoon phase. It is in the long-term relationship
that our capacity to maintain the vitality and energy of love is challenged. The challenge goes beyond simply getting along. There are lots
of couples who get along but whose relationship lacks passion. Some of
these couples have excluded anything controversial from their relationship in an effort to keep the peace. It is a peace that comes with a price.

In my view, not being truly open because it may "stir things up" is
precisely the wrong thing to do. Passion, I believe, comes from being
emotionally open in a relationship and allowing the other person to do

the same. Being open requires that we make our feelings known when we talk about things that are important to us and that we stay emotionally connected to our love partner when he or she thinks, feels, and believes differently; we don't waste our energy trying to change or fix each other.

Yes, creating and maintaining a vibrant love by revealing yourself, warts and all, can be a frightening prospect. However, to do otherwise, to avoid the risk of being open, or to discourage your partner's openness because it doesn't conform to your views is the biggest risk of all. It will, with certainty, drain the relationship and leave it empty. The excitement of the early days will become a distant memory to be mourned. The face that excited, the touch that electrified, the personality that stimulated will become merely comfortable, like the living-room sofa. This is so because the liveliness of love relationships, the very core energy of love, is fed by the openness that comes from the heart, talking about our inner lives.

Indeed, every experienced couple therapist will tell you that openness is at the root of the strongest love relationships. We also know that deception in all its forms is the enemy of a rich and vibrant love because it is the antithesis of openness. Deception is a tough and tricky enemy. The training starts innocently enough with the little white lies of childhood. We learn about white lies from our parents, peers, neighbors, and the other adults surrounding us.

We see tears streaming down Mommy's face and we ask, "What's the matter?" Mommy responds, "Nothing, I'm fine." The phone rings and Mommy answers. Dad signals to her and whispers, "Tell him I'm not here." We hear Mom and Dad bad-mouthing their friends Fred and Andrea Johnson. "He's boring and monotone; she's self-centered and grandiose." And then the Johnsons come over and we observe our parents greet them as if they are best friends. "Oh, we've really been looking forward to seeing you. . . ."

Because we are easily influenced as children, it is not long before—whether our motives are well intentioned or not, conscious or well guarded—deception becomes part of our existence. It wears countless faces and sometimes, like a seasoned actor, it transforms to the point of slipping into our lives barely noticed. That is a dangerous deception, the kind that enters our lives unnoticed. Then there is the type of deception that jumps out at us in headlines. At times it seems as if examples of blatant deception are everywhere, erosive factors that undercut the very foundation of authenticity. Consider these examples:

Whether they want to be or not, sports figures, those men and women who are paid multimillions for their athletic prowess, are role models for children and many adults. But barely a month goes by without some incident. Someone gets arrested, gets caught in some sexually compromising incident, or goes into rehab. The same thing occurs with the men and women whose music we admire and the actors whose images we watch on TV and in movie theaters. Sure, they are just people, but they are people whose lives touch and influence ours. And what about world leaders? Some actually live lives that are admirable. However, many don't. Scandal, lies, and cover-ups are not uncommon. Being inundated with bigger-than-life people who fall from grace on a regular basis serves to integrate deception into our national psyche. *That's just the way real life is. . . .*

The news media influence our lives tremendously as well. With images and words we rely on, we form attitudes and perspectives on events and people. Yet even those that do the reporting have been deceptive. There have been repeated instances of reporters rushing to judgment and reporting incomplete, biased, or even fabricated stories. *After all, it is a competitive business, and getting the public's attention is where the money is. . . .*

We hear stories of high-achieving students who cut corners, cheat, and plagiarize. We may feel a mixture of sadness and relief—sadness at the loss of vicarious innocence we experience and relief that our own corner-cutting sins are diminished. It seems that every year a biography of a revered person comes out and reveals that the person is not whom we thought he or she was but is in fact someone else, someone with a closet filled with skeletons. Most of us have heard of doctors who cover up medical mistakes, lawyers who stretch honesty and ethics to win their cases, and scientists who fake data to promote their career. These are people many of us look up to; we count on them to be forthright. *If they can't lead lives of virtue, what chance do we stand?*

Repeatedly, businesspeople use deceptive strategies, even outright lies, when that behavior serves their interest to get ahead. Recent examples include pharmaceutical companies rushing to market with a dangerous drug, influenced by its enormous profit potential; car and tire manufacturers withholding information about faulty products; major corporations hiding their losses with accounting firms that collude in the scheme; charities giving more to themselves than to the needy; and companies clandestinely dumping pollutants into our environment to avoid costly waste-management expenditures.

Advertisements, whether in print, on radio, or on television, are meant to sell product. It's called putting the best face forward. However, deception is such an integral part of the process, we barely give it any thought. It is not what we are told in ads, it is what we are *not* told that is deceptive. And when we are told it is because law, as in drug ads, requires it. I am thinking of the ads for prescription drugs that address various illnesses and include the side effects of the medication in a tone that makes it seem as if they are minor. However, if you listen closely, it seems you may be better off with the illness than the "cure."

Our government deceives us—telling us this or that program will help us but leaving out whom it will hurt. Our politicians lie, and lie about lying. Our police have been known to lie, sometimes on the witness stand. Religious leaders offer hope on occasions when there is no hope. Educators lie by scattering blame for a student's failure on everyone but themselves. Parents lie. Deception abounds and nobody admits it.

For physicians, the question of being candid about a patient's serious illness comes up frequently. There was a time when standard medical practice was to avoid giving the patient a grave diagnosis. While this trend has changed in recent years—probably due to the fear of lawsuits—people couldn't even count on candor in the final phase of their lives. And perhaps some, so used to not dealing with the truth, didn't even want candor in their last days.

We live in a world that challenges our integrity at every turn. And it is not just the headlines that bombard us, nor is it something that occurs only with other people. In our daily love lives in small ways that affect us powerfully we are challenged with the dilemma of facing an uncomfortable authenticity or sliding into a familiar deception on a regular basis. Have you ever told a "white lie" to avoid an argument with your spouse? What about lowering the price of a purchase—especially of a purchase you realize was unnecessary or overboard? Or covering up for the kids? Or denying that you find someone else attractive? If you have answered affirmatively to any of these questions, you have a lot of company. A poll of one thousand married couples interviewed separately and published in *Reader's Digest* (Lague 2001) confirms that truth isn't faring well in marriage. Dishonesty is emerging as the rule rather than the exception. These small breaches of honesty may have a minor impact if they are isolated, but over time repeated instances have a cumulative effect. And repeated instances of deception, unfortunately, are not uncommon.

Most of us are disappointed by a love partner as a result of an everyday event far more often than we are made angry or jealous by a serious and dramatic deception. For example, Phil still has a cigarette or two a day, in utter secrecy. His wife, Agnes, a nurse, has pleaded with him to stop. Her father died of lung cancer so it is no small issue to her. Phil has agreed but is undeterred. "I find a way," he says. "Cigarettes relax me. I make sure to smoke early in the day at work. I always carry a mouth spray. A couple of cigarettes are not going to harm me. If I told Agnes, she would raise the roof, so why aggravate her?" What else does Phil hide to avoid confrontations with Agnes? And what if Agnes was to discover Phil's deception? Does she sense he is being less than candid? If so, how does this affect the intimacy between them?

Here is how one woman, Margaret, married for sixteen years, was affected:

We were sitting down for dinner at a restaurant while on vacation. I was very happy, and I assumed that Mike was as well. When I told him how happy I was with him and with life in general he just looked at me in silence. "Is something wrong?" I asked. Once again he paused. Then he told me that he was dreadfully unhappy. Not with me, thank goodness, but with everything else in his life. He didn't like working for the family business, he didn't like that he couldn't lose the extra pounds, he hated our friends, and he wasn't happy with where we lived. It blew me away. I had never heard any of this. I thought he was as happy as I was! If I hadn't asked, he would have just continued to hide all this from me. He says he didn't want to worry me. Now I wonder what else he isn't honest about. I just feel that I can't count on what he says.

While Margaret's reaction is common, she is not beyond deception herself. Margaret has been a "closet" drinker for years. Her security has been assaulted, despite her own long-standing deception. When there is deception in one area, the disappointed partner is often so shaken that the shock waves ripple throughout the relationship—despite his or her own honesty shortcomings. The result is that the deceived is left wondering if he or she will be able to feel secure with that person again. That is the power of deception; particularly in a love relationship, it can crumble the foundation of security that is essential if intimacy is to prosper. Dishonesty spreads like a deadly toxin throughout the entire relationship.

For instance, Harold and Carol, who have lived together for the past few years, are on the verge of splitting up because Carol contends that Harold "never lives up to his word." Here's what Carol has to say about some troubling events:

Harold is a contractor, and he lies to his customers all the time. They call the house and complain to me. In fairness, I can't argue with their position. He is unreliable, he makes promises he doesn't keep, and he takes shortcuts with the work. I know they are right because he does the same thing with me and it has undermined the closeness between us. I just don't want to open myself to someone who can't be counted on.

As Carol describes it, when she complained to Harold about his behavior, their conversation went like this:

HAROLD: *I have a lot of demands on me. I try to make people happy, but I guess you can't please everyone all the time.*

CAROL: *So now you tell me that you are really just a straight-arrow guy who is trying to please everyone. You expect me to buy that? You expect me to believe that you are just a misguided Santa?*

HAROLD: *I'm just saying that sometimes I have so much to deal with that I say yes to get some relief.*

CAROL: (sarcastically) *That's great. And when the time comes to put up? More lies and excuses to get relief?*

A relationship like the one between Carol and Harold can continue, but it is more a pseudorelationship than anything else. Neither Carol nor Harold is open about anything important. Carol is disappointed by and insecure about Harold's lack of candor and is no longer confident in his honesty in any area of their life together. Harold is rationalizing and denying his deception.

In couple therapy it became clear as Carol and Harold worked toward a resolution that Harold had chosen the convenience of "yessing" people just the way he had seen his father deal with his mother and the other people in his life. By talking openly for the first time, they began to establish a renewed intimacy with each other. Rather than hide the real and show the false, thereby threatening the survival of their relationship, they began to speak truthfully, but as we will see, that isn't as easy as it may seem. Lying is only one form of deception, perhaps the easiest to recognize and address. There are many other ways to be deceptive, and some of them include being self-deceptive. Because of the enormous human capacity for self-deception, we may fail to recognize when we are not living authentically and truly.

How, specifically, do we engage in deception? As we have seen, we lie outright, with the intention of convincing the other person of what we know is not true. We tell ourselves that our lack of candor is irrelevant, not worth notice. We also withhold; in this instance it is not what we say, but what we don't say that undermines intimacy. We are faced with a choice on a daily basis: do we say how we *really* feel, what we are *really* thinking, or do we play it safe? For many of us, it is the safe route that is most traveled. Ironically, that is the route that we disdain when we see politicians taking it. "He's just being political," we say with contempt.

What harm will a little white lie do? That is a question that may not even cross your mind. Sadly, most of us are so used to cutting corners with our honesty that the question no longer enters our consciousness. Whether we acknowledge it or not, whether we lie to ourselves about our lying or do it with conscious intent and purpose, deception stands in the way of lovers knowing themselves and others. We often compound the lack of candor by giving a benevolent explanation for deception, contending that it's for the other person's sake. We think or tell our partner, "I'm doing it to protect you, to make you feel better." It sounds altruistic, but deceivers really protect only themselves. The protection also comes with side effects: in most cases the deceived partner knows or has a hunch that the truth is not being told. As a result, an invisible wall of suspicion separates the partners.

The Blame Game

Outright lies, rationalizations and all, are just the tip of the iceberg, the most easily recognizable form of deception; we also depart from truth telling in ways that are not typically viewed as dishonest. Take blame, for example. Blame is epidemic in love relationships. In fact, in some relationships blame becomes the predominant theme. As any couple therapist can testify, the aggrieved partner in a troubled relationship knows who the culprit is; all that remains is enlightenment, making the other person see his or her fault, thereby taking responsibility off oneself and becoming the victim, free of fault.

It is comforting to feel free of fault. It feels empowering to firmly put oneself in the "one-up" position while assigning the other person the "one-down" position. However, it is a false and dishonest victory. I have rarely seen a couple whose conflict was completely one-sided, that is, where one person was the villain wearing the black hat and the other person was wearing the pure white hat of the innocent. One thing is certain: pointing the finger at the other person allows you to avoid your own issues and your responsibility in the conflict. Witness the following:

A couple has a fight. It begins because the wife feels irritated with her husband about something. They go to bed that evening without saying a word to each other. She is no longer angry and would like her husband to make contact with her—talk to her, reach out to her, caress her. He, not knowing that her mood has passed and fearing that she is still upset, does nothing of the sort, deciding to wait until she gives him some indication that she will respond more kindly. She is not willing to reach out and make contact herself, although she would love to do so. Lying there, she begins to blame him for "not making a move," for not doing something she herself is unwilling to do.

Why doesn't she reach out to her husband? She fears being rejected. While she blames him for not reaching out, she is not taking responsibility for her own fear. What's more, whatever they fought about earlier was not one-sided. Either partner could go back to that conflict and simply state his or her part without pointing the finger at the other partner.

Here's another example:

A husband is a very poor manager of money. His debts pile up unpaid. His one major avenue to recovery is to file for a substantial federal income tax refund dating back several years. He procrastinates despite his wife's pleading. The bills continue to pile up, adding more pressure to the couple's tensions. Finally, the husband files for the refund and receives a prompt reply from the Internal Revenue Service stating that his request exceeded the cutoff date and was no longer valid. He immediately blames his wife, saying she should have "kept after him." When she grows angry and tells him that his broken promise to get things done has hurt her, he continues to deny personal responsibility and escalates the blame to a new level. "If it was that important to you," he says, "why didn't you lock me out of the house or something until I filed the return?" I suppose the wife could have taken the kind of dramatic action her husband proposed; however, that wasn't the intention of his suggestion. His intention was to blame her for the dilemma, to shift responsibility to her and away from himself.

In the previous examples, the blamer has the attitude, "I'm not responsible, you are!" From this follows, "If you are responsible for my (our) discomfort, distress, or unhappiness, only you can alter it." In all of these instances the blamer is being dishonest in an effort to avoid responsibility for his or her behavior. What's more, there is an inherent assumption that the blamer is powerless and therefore at the mercy of the other partner. Unless the circumstance is very unusual, like being held at gunpoint, adults are rarely powerless.

When couples relate in such a blame-oriented way, they create a major obstacle to being open and real with each other. Not only are they being dishonest with each other—pointing their finger outward rather than looking inward at their part in their difference—nothing is resolved if the focus is on screaming or silently sulking about who is to blame. Resolution is unlikely unless one partner or preferably both are willing to take the initiative. Both must drop the victim role. Neither is powerless, they are just acting that way, and by pointing outward they are avoiding a confrontation with their own issues. That's basically dishonest.

Not only are love partners dishonestly avoiding their part in a dispute by resorting to blame, typically, in the blame-counterblame pattern both partners issue their complaints after the unwanted behavior has occurred but do nothing while it is taking place. It is like playing a game of "Gotcha!" A husband may accuse his wife of being inconsiderate because she repeatedly interrupts him. He will nag, complain, sulk, and admonish, but rarely will he take a firm stand while the behavior is actually happening. He could take a stand while being interrupted by stating, "You're interrupting me, Barbara. Please let me finish what I'm saying." If this didn't work, he might simply get up and leave the room, saying, "It seems, by your constant interruptions, that you are not interested in what I am saying. When you feel more like listening, let me know." Although this behavior may seem harsh, it is honest and direct—and more effective than repeated and empty complaints. It is a matter of giving credibility to what is being said.

Susan harbors resentment toward Bill because he doesn't pay attention to her at social gatherings. Yet this behavior has continued on Bill's part for a long period of time, so it is likely that Susan has been blaming and antagonizing him rather than taking responsibility for getting what she wants: more attention. Perhaps she goes off in a corner at parties to sulk or becomes nasty and sarcastic about Bill's social adroitness. Later, when they are alone, she may withdraw or explode and tell Bill his behavior made her furious. Her comments will then escalate their conflict into a fight or mutual withdrawal.

If Susan would take responsibility for her shyness, envy of her husband's social popularity, or desire for more attention instead of waiting for him to "save" her, she would be approaching her own issues honestly, rather than hiding behind her complaints. This might involve a total cessation of blame, working to overcome her social shyness, and making a concerted effort to be part of her husband's conversations instead of withdrawing from them and stewing. In fact, if she did nothing to work on her social shyness but simply declared it rather than blaming her husband, it would restore honesty around this issue.

How do you know when blame is coming your way? Contrast the following statements:

"You don't love me."	*"I wish I could feel loved by you."*
"You make me nervous."	*"I am afraid."*
"You make me mad."	*"I am angry at you."*
"You are too bossy."	*"I hate when you tell me*
	what to do."

"You" statements are actually "I" statements in disguise. If an individual is upset, it is easy for him or her to avoid ownership of his or her feelings by indicating "It's your fault!" "You" statements are essential to the blaming game. When sentences begin with "you," the speaker's part in any difference or dissension is omitted. When the sentence begins with "I," there is an acknowledgment of personal responsibility; it is harder to put all the blame on the listener—and it is a more honest statement.

What Is It You're Really Saying?

Just as pointing a finger at a love partner, hiding behind blame, and playing the victim rather than being open about your own issues are forms
of deception, so is indirect communication. Communication may be
straightforward and factual—"I want to eat" or "I put gas in the car" or
"It is cold." However, sometimes indirectness and subtlety play a major
role in a relationship. In these instances something is wanted—be it
change, clarification, reassurance, companionship, or support—but it is
approached manipulatively rather than directly.

Doreen and Ralph have been married for twelve years. They were
both married before. When Ralph was still married to his first wife, he
was arrested for selling marijuana. He still smokes on occasion, and
Doreen even joins him. Lately he has had a lot of extra cash. Being in
the restaurant business, he simply explained to Doreen that things had
been going well. However, she has been getting hang-up calls, and his
cell phone bills have skyrocketed. Doreen has not questioned him about
this, but she suspects that he has gone back to dealing. She has stopped
at the restaurant and it has been quiet rather than very busy as Ralph
maintains. The more she looks into this, the more he seems to cover up,
but she has not come out and made an accusation. She is simply inves-
tigating. Consequently, their discussions about his longer-than-usual
absences from home, his business issues, and the mysterious phone calls
are filled with misunderstanding:

DOREEN: *You know what, I think I'll come into the restaurant and
start helping out there.*

RALPH: *That's OK, Doreen. I'm doing well with the way things are
managed. I don't really need you there.*

DOREEN: (disappointed) *Oh, then I can keep you company.*

RALPH: (starting to experience a vague sense of guilt) *Doreen, it's
nice of you to want to be with me, but my schedule keeps me busy
from nine in the morning to very late. I would hardly have time for
you. Besides, it would take time away from the kids.*

DOREEN: (persistent with a trace of annoyance in her voice) *I think I'd like to help out anyway.*

RALPH: (with impatience and annoyance) *Listen, I don't need you, the other employees may resent you, and I would hardly see you, so there's no point. Let's leave it at that.*

DOREEN: *Let's not leave it at that. I'm coming in!*

RALPH: (angrily and with frustration) *Shit! Doreen, for Christ's sake, when you get so damned unreasonable, I feel as if I don't know you anymore. You're not the woman I married.*

DOREEN: (her anxiety and resentment escalating) *That's it! You're hiding something. I knew it!*

Conversations based on indirectness such as Doreen and Ralph's are frequently disastrous. In this instance, Ralph assumes Doreen is merely being pigheaded. Doreen, of course, assumes Ralph, cornered, is purposely evasive. Had she directly stated her concern (or had Ralph asked her why working at the restaurant was so important), the outcome might have been very different. These patterns of behavior are somewhat present in almost all relationships: there is an argument whose source is camouflaged, the result after many futile bouts is often of the you-hurt-me-so-I'll-hurt-you variety, and, in many instances, vindictiveness becomes the major force in the gradual weakening of the relationship.

As the negativity created by indirectness escalates, it spills over into other areas of the relationship; that is, once a negative, destructive atmosphere of misunderstanding has been established, more indirectness and misunderstanding are likely to follow. Ralph may get offhand questions about his whereabouts or his finances or his phone bills and start covering his tracks, which will lead to more suspicion. Doreen is fearful of confronting Ralph; instead she is caught in a series of deceptive, relationship-defeating attempts to allay her anxiety while avoiding a straightforward and honest discussion of her concern.

In couple therapy, as Dr. Paul Watzlawick and his associates describe in their book *Change,* one frequently sees both partners caught in a futile push-pull based on indirectly expressed statements. For instance, a wife may have the impression that her husband is not open enough for her to know where she stands with him, what is going on in his head, what he is doing when he is away from home, and so on. Quite naturally, she will therefore attempt to make herself more secure by asking him questions, watching his behavior, and checking on him in a variety of ways. He is likely to consider her behavior intrusive and react by withholding information that in and of itself would be quite harmless and irrelevant, "just to teach her that I am not a child in need of checking."

Rather than making her back down, her husband's reaction increases her insecurity and provides further fuel for her worries: "If he does not talk to me about even these little things, he *must* be hiding something." The less information he gives her, the more persistently she will seek it; the more she seeks it, the less he will give her. It is not long before the drama evolves to a point that Dr. Watzlawick views as reminiscent of two sailors hanging out of either side of a sailboat in order to steady it: the more the one leans overboard, the more the other has to hang out to compensate for the instability created by the other's attempts at stabilizing the boat, while the boat itself would be quite steady if not for the insecurities of its passengers.

It is predictable that unless something changes in this situation—the couple discusses their issues openly and explicitly—the occupants of the boat—the love boat, as it were—will be under constant unnecessary strain or, worse yet, end up in the water. A direct and pointed statement by one of the partners may not in fact *resolve* a relationship issue. It may, however, clarify the underlying issue. The couple may even conclude that they are at a temporary impasse; that is, they may agree that they disagree on some issue. This recognition, although it may seem limited, is a start. It is preferable to the undercurrent of torment and nagging uncertainty that accompanies deceptive obfuscation.

Many requests are not expressed openly and directly. Often we don't want to take responsibility for our requests, so we hide and disguise them in questions, hints, obscure suggestions, and countless other manipulations, all in an effort to satisfy our desires without the risk of being rejected.

Open requests require an awareness of our desires and involve several risks. The first is an acknowledgment that the other person has something to offer that is of value. This recognition poses a particular threat to couples engaged in a power struggle. By asking in a disguised form, the asker "discounts" the partner's power. Second, the asker risks being asked to reciprocate. Doubting one's willingness or capacity to satisfy the other's requests, one may prefer to stay self-contained rather than being reciprocal. Finally, there is a risk of rejection. Many of us have a fear of the word *no*, and by being vague, we hope to temper the pain of refusal.

The problem with requests that are camouflaged, as with all indirect messages, is that those requests that are not understood are less likely to be satisfied. What's more, resentment often accompanies the unmet desire and is expressed in disguised form through nagging, criticism, and other kinds of annoyances and frustrations. Ultimately, the opportunity for a deeper understanding—whether of a refusal or of a request—is lost, and along with it the intimacy is diminished.

And There's More . . .

Practically all social relationships involve agreements—whether official or unofficial, tacit or explicit. Agreements govern the ways in which people behave toward each other. In couple relationships, where contact is frequent and covers a wide variety of behaviors, agreements are particularly important. Ironically, some of those that are most potent are those that are hidden. They are made with little or no conscious awareness.

Witness the coupling of a shy person with a very outgoing person. When these two joined they made an implicit agreement. The shy person had found someone who would carry on the social interaction, and the outgoing person had found someone who seemed to be the strong silent type that offset his or her chattering. Another hidden agreement is formed between the emotionally expressive and the more cognitive per-

son. It is a wedding of the heart and mind. Each feels the other is bringing a balance to the relationship. However, somewhere down the marital
road, one or the other is inevitably going to want to modify the agreement. Usually, one or both are disillusioned with the original "deal." This
could present difficulties because the agreement was never acknowledged
in the first place. Each partner feels wronged and somehow cheated, but
typically neither is willing to take a look at the deal he or she entered; each
is too invested in announcing that he or she got the short end.

Some types of relationship "contracts," as agreements are often called,
are drawn up with no intention of carrying them out. One type that
wreaks havoc on the emotional security of a couple and that inhibits
openness involves making an offer that is withdrawn when the partner
accepts. For example, one partner may feel pressured by the other to
spend more time together so he or she may reluctantly suggest that he
or she will take a day off so that they can spend some time together. The
initiating partner is hoping that the offer will be appreciated but
declined. However, the other partner, pleased by the offer, readily
accepts. Acceptance is then met with an accusation: "How could you be
so unconcerned with my career to encourage my absence from work?"
Or, in a variation on this, one partner may offer an agreement only to
negotiate it *after* the other has accepted it. The experience is not unlike
purchasing an item only to find—after reading the small print—that
the item isn't what was represented.

Yet another deceptive ploy casts a long-lasting negative spell on a couple. In this instance, one person suggests that cooperation can be
expected. But somehow the cooperation never occurs or it occurs in a
different and unacceptable form. That is, the partner behaves inconsid-
erately while appearing to be considerate and collaborative. This creates
a growing expectation than can slowly drive the expectant partner to
distraction. Here's an example:

KATHY: *I need help tonight getting the room ready for my book
discussion group.*

FRANK: (with a show of concern) *No problem. Let me know what
you want, and I'll take care of it.*

KATHY: *I just need you to move some of the heavy furniture so I can arrange for us to sit in a circle.*

FRANK: *OK, I'll do that. Now, what's for lunch?*

Frank is busy all day, and Kathy worries that he will forget. When it comes time for her group, Frank helps put out the food and takes an interest in the book they are going to discuss, and then he disappears without moving the furniture! Later, when Kathy questions him, he maintains that he did help—he brought out the food and even took interest in the book to be discussed. Frank feels he is being "ragged," and Kathy feels confused. A dull ache is beginning between her shoulder blades and moving toward the back of her neck. How could these unsettled feelings relate to such a sweet, caring partner? Kathy is likely to conclude, "There is something wrong with me." In reality, the experience at home was not unlike reaching into a fog. Her husband responded, but not to the issue that Kathy needed.

Deception, as we have seen, is more than outright lies. Deception is also blame in various guises, a variety of ways to camouflage real feelings and requests by indirect statements, and agreements that are not really agreements. All are dishonest. And then there is what is withheld. We do not ask an essential question or make a remark that clarifies an issue. Rather than be open, we play it safe and do not express how we really feel and what we think. We withhold pertinent information from our partner. We do not say, "There are some things about this I am not comfortable talking about." Rather, we give the impression that we have been completely forthcoming. In fact, many of us rationalize our withholding by calling it "privacy" when in actuality there is more to it. Privacy is a right to separateness that all of us have; withholding pertinent information from a love partner is not privacy, it is deliberate concealment.

Most often withholding occurs gradually and is the result of an interactive process. John doesn't bring up issues for discussion because he finds Mary too critical of him. Mary is then critical of John's silence. John then concludes that he was right about Mary all along: she is too judgmental.

Sometimes a partner will encourage openness and then discourage it by frequent interruption or critically challenging remarks, prompting the speaker to think, "Anything I say may—and will—be used against me." Often, even the statement, "We need to talk" takes on an emotional tone and is interpreted ominously: "Uh oh, he (she) wants to complain about me again."

Yet another subtle deception comes in the form of questions. The purpose of questions is to obtain information, but questions also direct attention to the other person and tend to put him or her on the defensive. "Do you have another woman?" risks a defensive answer and futile argument. But "There's something missing in our relationship, and I would like to talk about it" is the question converted into a statement. The statement emphasizes the speaker's responsibility for his or her position rather than allowing it to remain hidden behind the question.

As with "you" statements mentioned earlier, questions are often accusations. A man asks his partner, "Where did you go? Who were you with? Why are you driving so fast? Why are you wearing that blouse?" When unscrambled, these are all subtle forms of criticism. This is particularly the case if the question begins with "why": "Why shouldn't I think of myself? Why can't you remember my messages? Why are you so uptight? Why are you wearing that jacket?"

Each of these questions is a thinly concealed criticism that reinforces the speaker in a "one-up" position, holding the listener "one-down." Each is unanswerable because it implies the listener has done something wrong and demands that he or she justify or alter the behavior. Rather than increasing openness, most "why" questions begin an endless exchange of rationalizations and explanations that move a couple further and further from intimacy.

Sometimes questions are traps that spring once the respondent has committed him- or herself. "When did you get home?" asks a man in an apparently innocent request for information. But if the man already knows that his partner came home late and is angry she didn't call, then the question is not so innocent; it is a deceitful, vague expression of a feeling: "I know you came home late last night, and I'm angry that you didn't call to inform me" or, "I want you to show me that you care by calling, and I'm hurt that you didn't." As it stood, the intent of the question was manipulative. If the response is honest, it gives the angry man "permission" to show his anger; and if the response is a lie, it offers him an opportunity to begin the game of "I gotcha."

Some Suggestions for Increasing Honesty

We all lie for the usual reasons: to make ourselves comfortable at the moment, to escape disapproval and censure, to avoid complexity and complication, to keep our emotions at bay. All relationships, and particularly love relationships, are stunted by lies. Telling the truth—being open about what you feel and think—is the foundation of authenticity, self-regard, intimacy, and integrity. Simply put, love requires honesty; lying erodes love. Lies come in various forms: the outright lies of commission and the harder to detect lies of omission. Then there are less obvious forms of deception. Here are some suggestions for countering them:

- As we have seen, casting blame in love relationships is basically dishonest. To avoid blame, consider beginning your statements with a form of the pronoun *I* (*me, my, mine*). "I" statements are expressions of responsibility; beginning a sentence with "I" personalizes your feelings or thoughts. Note that tacking a prefix like "I think that you . . ." or "I feel that you . . ." onto a sentence does not make it an "I" statement. An "I" statement is a report of your awareness of yourself, not the other person: "I wish I felt loved by you" rather than "I feel that you don't love me."

- To further increase the benefits of self-statements, it is important that they be present-oriented. This requires limiting your personal observations to the present tense ("That bothers me" rather than "That could be disturbing") and to immediate experience ("I see you staring into space and not responding to my questions" rather than "You never pay attention to me").

When something is wanted—be it change, clarification, reassurance, companionship, or support—it is important that the message be direct and to the point, not camouflaged and manipulative.

- Here is an experience that will help you be more direct and honest in your requests. Sit facing your partner. It is important to maintain eye contact. Making some kind of physical contact as well is likely to deepen the involvement and increase the probability of learning something about your partner and yourself.

  Each partner is to alternate making requests. Taking turns, begin each sentence with "I want you to . . ." Be very specific about your request. Avoid generalities such as "I want you to please me." State in detail *how* and *when* you would like to be pleased. For example, "I want you to kiss me when I come home from work." The listening partner is not to reply to these requests. Take turns expressing requests for a total of five minutes.

  Now take another few minutes each and summarize your understanding of your partner's requests. Clear up any misunderstanding, but do not express agreement or disagreement with a particular request. The emphasis here is on understanding, on assuring your partner that the message sent is the message received. When mutual understanding has been achieved, discuss your feelings about each other's requests. Which of your own requests are really important to you? Which of your partner's requests are you desirous of meeting, and which are you reluctant or unwilling to meet?

  Follow up this discussion with an actual request. Note the wording being suggested for making requests: (1) begin with "I," (2) be specific, and (3) use "want" ("desire," "prefer," "like") rather than "need." A want is something that is desired but not necessary. "Need" implies that something is critical to survival, which is hardly ever the case in request making.

- Here is another experience. This one will increase your awareness of how you slip past difficult situations. In this experience, one partner is to request something that his or her partner is *unwilling* to grant. Make this request repeatedly. With each repetition, the unwilling partner is to say "no" without actually saying "no" (e.g., "I'll think about it"; "Let's discuss it later"). Be aware of the nature of the evasions. Continue for about four minutes, switch places, and resume for another four minutes. After both partners have had a turn being the requester and the evader, discuss the experience. What did you learn about your own and your partner's ways of avoiding a direct "no"?

Questions, as we have seen, can also mask personal reactions. Certainly not all questions are illegitimate, manipulative devices; in fact there are two specific circumstances in which questions can be very useful in personal conversations: (1) when feedback is wanted ("What's your reaction?"), and (2) for clarification ("I'm not sure I understand. Do you mean . . . ?").

- In the interest of taking responsibility for your own position or preference, before asking a question of an intimate, attempt to convert it into a statement. When questions are asked, they should be preceded by a self-statement. For example, Julie might ask Walter if he has plans for Saturday afternoon. A "yes" from Walter may provoke an outburst from Julie in which she accuses him of always making plans without her. On the other hand, a "no" is likely to be accompanied by an apprehension on Walter's part that he is about to commit himself before he knows to what. In contrast, if Julie were to take responsibility for her message first (e.g., "I am going shopping tomorrow afternoon") and then ask her question (e.g., "Would you like to come with me?"), Walter would not feel as if he had been set up.

Life is complicated, messy, and full of dilemmas and contradictions. In a single conversation, you may be truthful, deceptive, and partially truthful—sometimes without noticing. Following the previous suggestions will help you increase your awareness and allow truth telling to become a powerful way of enriching your love.

2

THE OPENNESS SCALE

HOW OPEN ARE YOU?

In the abstract, people almost unanimously applaud honesty, which, as popular wisdom suggests, is "the best policy." But when we move away from abstract values and focus instead on specific incidents in the lives of real people, "the best policy" is not easily applied.

It is so easy to get caught up in being who others want you to be. Rationalization abounds; convincing yourself that what you believe and feel is somehow not acceptable to disclose comes naturally. Most of us have been brought up and surrounded with maxims like these: "What he doesn't know won't hurt him." "The best thing may be not to tell her." "She doesn't really need to know." "He has enough to worry about." It is tempting to play it safe. Nonetheless, a choice that confronts us at every moment in a love relationship is this: how open are we going to be; how much of ourselves are we going to reveal?

For too many of us, past experience dictates caution. For some, having felt the piercing hurt of being judged by those closest to us, we don't want to reexperience it. For others, we anticipate hurt because of the war that we've seen between the most influential people in our lives—

our parents. Yet others have simply never learned what real openness is about. Being guarded has become a natural state. Still others feel that if they were revealing of themselves they would be found wanting. In all cases, whether we realize it or not, we camouflage our true selves as protection against criticism or rejection. The protection, however, comes at a steep price.

Those of us who do not reveal ourselves, especially to the person we are coupled with, tend to lose touch with our real selves. Oscar Combs, a forty-three-year-old journalist, knows this feeling well. Depressed for many months, out of desperation he decided to consult with a psychologist. Now, three months after a yearlong therapy experience, he wrote me this letter about his struggle with being open:

> At first the idea of psychological help seemed strange to me. I wondered, "How can this help me—just talking about things that are personal?" But I found that talking, having to voice my thoughts, forced me to deal with things I had been avoiding for a very long time. As we continued to meet, I spoke more easily of my relationship with my wife, Mary. In our conversations I became aware that all these years were spent avoiding involvement with her. I really had no intimacy; after seventeen years of marriage, I wasn't close to her or to anyone else. If Mary was getting too close, I busied myself with work, limiting the amount of time I spent with her; even if I revealed a personal feeling, I did so in a controlled manner, making sure not to be too revealing. Basically, I had this feeling that if Mary, or anyone else for that matter, really got to know me, I would be a total disappointment. I guess I don't have much value in myself as a person.
>
> At one of my sessions I remarked that I haven't let myself really be loved by anyone. The statement was true and it was agonizing, but there was still a buffer between the words and my experience. It wasn't quite real; it didn't penetrate my armor. You asked me to repeat my statement slowly and as I did so to focus on my feelings. I did it once and started to feel weak; I felt wobbly even though I was seated. You asked me to do it again, and I tried but I could barely speak. I felt more deeply disturbed than I could describe; I had reached a point far

away from anything that I had ever known. Despair, fear, and grief, all greater than I had felt before, were evoked by the thought of how insulated from love I had made myself. I was engulfed in emotion beyond anything I had ever experienced.

As soon as the session ended, I went home and forced myself to sleep. I was scared and unhappy when I woke up. I couldn't rid myself of the thought that I had withdrawn from significant human contacts; I was not even intimate with myself. I would not allow myself to experience my feelings about myself, and I managed to avoid dealing with anything "real" with those closest to me, especially Mary. For the first time since childhood I felt real panic. Over time you encouraged me gently but persistently to risk being open, to let myself experience my feelings, and to expose them. Gradually, I was able to reveal more of my "true self" to Mary. That's when my depression started to lift. It was as if a load had been removed from my back.

Not only does openness help lift depression and counter loneliness, it revitalizes intimacy. Couples who have cut off the most intimate areas of their relationship are all too apparent—they are the ones looking bored in the restaurant after the gossip and talk about the children has been spent. Are you one of those couples? Check the Openness Scale and find out.

Measuring Your Level of Self-Disclosure

The Openness Scale is most helpful when you and your partner answer the questions separately and then compare your responses. It is designed to be a basis for discussion with your partner about the level of self-disclosure between you. It is not a precise scientific instrument. (A brief scale can't capture all of the nuances involved.)

To use the scale, read each statement and indicate how well it applies to your self-disclosure behavior. Then add up the numbers to get your total openness score, and look at your overall pattern of responses. Compare this to your partner's score and pattern of responses. This will give you a picture of the overall level of openness in your relationship, as well as the areas in which it is strongest and weakest. (Discussion on interpreting your scores follows at the end of the scale.)

THE OPENNESS SCALE

Rate the likelihood of being open in your relationship for each of the following situations according to the point system given. Don't take time to think about each response; just put down the first reaction that comes to mind. You will have a chance to review your responses after you complete the scale, and then you can compare and discuss your responses with your partner.

0—not a chance
1—possibly
2—likely
3—almost certainly

1. There is a controversial issue on the news. It is not merely something abstract like your senator announcing increased funding for improving rural roadways. It is more personal like the debate over abortion rights, the death penalty, or the decriminalization of drug use. Your views are much different on the issue than your partner's views. Will you voice your views and explain why you feel as you do?

2. You had a bad day. Nothing went right. The boss gave you a hard time, a lot of it being justified; you almost had an accident on the way home because you weren't paying attention; and you slipped outside the house and nearly broke your neck. When you come in your partner asks you about your day. Do you give a full accounting?

3. You and your partner get into a bitter argument. Later on, after you've cooled down, you acknowledge to yourself that some of the things your partner said to you had merit and that some of what you said was defensive and mean-spirited. You can let the effects of the argument blow over, or you can confront the

issues that you've acknowledged and share them with your partner. How likely is it that you will take the path of confrontation?

4. Recently you have had a complete physical. Your partner has been on your case to take better care of yourself, and your physician feels the same way. Your blood pressure was too high, as were your cholesterol and blood sugar levels. You were told that you have to exercise more, lose weight, and manage stress more effectively. When you return home your partner asks you how the physical went. How likely is it that you will report the results fully and accurately?

5. You and your friend had a falling out. This was a close friendship, and as you've reviewed the relationship you realize that you've made some mistakes. Part of the basis for the falling out was due to unresolved issues of your own that got in the way. Your partner has, on occasion, pointed out these same issues. Will you go into detail about what happened between you and your friend and acknowledge your part in it?

6. Your partner does something without malice that nonetheless hurts your feelings deeply. Perhaps it was revealing something personal about you to a good friend, trading insults with you in the heat of anger, or giving you "constructive criticism" that touched something sensitive. Will you discuss your hurt feelings with your partner?

7. Your thoughts turn to something that you feel ashamed and guilty about—it might be about having mistreated someone, lying, or perhaps some unethical behavior like stealing. Do you share your thoughts with your partner?

8. You have been online glancing at some sexy websites as well as participating in some chat room discussions. Your partner asks you what you've been up to. How likely is it that you will give a full accounting of your activities?

9. Some things have occurred that have left you feeling really blue. It may have been being passed over for a promotion, it may have been a letdown on something that you were counting on, or perhaps it was a comment that someone made that really hit home and cut into your self-regard. Will you address the basis of your feelings with your partner?

10. You have an evaluation coming up at work, and you are anxious about the outcome. Your partner has been somewhat critical about your on-the-job attitude in the past. Your partner notices that you seem tense and asks you what's going on. Will you tell your partner about the upcoming sit-down with your boss and why you are anxious about it?

11. You are feeling the effects of a sexual slump with your partner. The basis may be boredom, it may be part of the natural fluctuation of interest that occurs in relationships, or perhaps it is more involved and sensitive. Will you share your thoughts and feelings on this issue with your partner?

12. There are some things that bother you about your partner. You don't want to go on the attack, but neither do you want to act like everything is fine. You are not sure how to approach the issues. One day your partner, who has sensed some undercurrent, asks you, "Are we OK?" How likely is it that you will begin a discussion about what's been bothering you?

13. On the way home from work you are thinking warmly about your partner. One particular incident stands out in your thoughts. It involved a situation where your partner was especially supportive and sensitive at a time when you felt very vulnerable. Your eyes fill with tears of gratitude as you review the kindness of your partner. When you arrive home, your partner greets you and asks you how you're doing. How likely is it that you will share the moving experience you had?

14. You get a call at work from an old friend whom your partner dislikes. You and your partner have argued about this before.

You defend your friend, but your partner feels your friend is a bad influence. After spending nearly an hour on the phone, you realize how much you miss your friend. Just after you hang up, your partner calls. "I've been trying to get through for nearly an hour," he (she) says. "Who were you on the phone with for so long?" How likely is it that you will tell your partner whom you were speaking with and how you felt about the call?

15. You are enjoying the experience of making love and feel very close to your partner. However, as is often the case, you are enhancing the lovemaking with fantasy. Your partner looks you in the eye, notices a distant gaze, and asks you what you are thinking about. Do you reveal your fantasy?

Interpretation

Now that you have completed the Openness Scale, add up your points. Your total score will range from 0 to 45. If you are in the group of high scorers, you are likely to feel that you are relatively free to be yourself with your partner. The lower your score, the more likely it is that you are cautious and guarded rather than open in your relationship. However, low scores should be viewed only as a signal that improvement is desirable, not as proof that the relationship is incurably dysfunctional. A more detailed interpretation of your score is as follows:

Watch Out! (0–15 points)

It is highly likely that you and your partner are very cautious and guarded with each other. Whether your motives are unconscious or intentional, deception is part of your everyday love-life existence. It wears countless faces and takes on an endless array of forms and functions. Most often you probably tell yourself that you are being less than open in the service of protecting your partner's feelings. While there is no doubt that altruism may play a part in your caution, it is you that you are actually protecting, not your partner. You have chosen peace at any price.

When you are silent or withholding, you may convince yourself that your failure to disclose is neutral or harmless. It is likely that we would all agree that we don't have to tell anyone everything. And that is true. Your life is not, nor should it be, an open book. But the more intimate you want your most valued relationship to be, the more you will need to reveal about your feelings and beliefs—and the bigger the emotional consequences of being guarded.

This isn't about privacy. We all need and value a degree of privacy. But your scores suggest a strong avoidance of openness that goes well beyond privacy. Privacy differs from deception. "Why start trouble?" obscures the full meaning and consequences of secrets and silence. Instead of intimacy we end up with a life in hiding in which we fail to know our partner and to be known. We fail to challenge ourselves to seek new truths and revise old ones.

Still Cautious After All These Years (16–30 points)

If you scored in the middle range, not as closed as those described previously but not as open as you might be, consider the following exchange:

SHE: *You never talk to me.*

HE: *What's on your mind?*

SHE: *It's not what's on my mind, it's that I never know what's on your mind.*

HE: *What do you want to know?*

SHE: *Everything!*

HE: *That's ridiculous.*

SHE: (angry) *I'll bet you don't think talking to that blonde assistant of yours is ridiculous!*

HE: *Aw, come on, cut it out.*

SHE: (on the verge of tears) *You never want to talk to me anymore the way you did when we were going together.*

HE: (rolling his eyes) *Here we go again.*

Does this exchange or some variation of it sound familiar? Your scores suggest that you can easily slip into this type of futile conversation. You are not alone. Lots of couples have this kind of interaction. It is fashionable these days for love partners to complain about their "communication." Husbands and wives accuse each other: "You never talk to me" or "You never listen to me."

Of course, the issue of real intimacy is larger than simply transmitting and receiving information. Real intimacy begins when your inner life is shared with your partner. This requires that you be in touch with your feelings and beliefs and that you make them explicit. The purpose of being open is to make the connection that achieves the *we* without damaging the *you* or *me*.

Your scores indicate that closeness is something that you desire but you also have serious reservations about exposing yourself. Perhaps being open has discouraged you. Maybe you ended up in a messy conflict, or something you said was thrown back at you, or you feel that your partner will back off if she or he *really* knows you. Many of us worry that if we fully disclose who we are, if we are transparent, we will be cast off. The fear of abandonment is very strong in all of us, and, if we allow it, it can paralyze us emotionally.

Intimacy Is Within Sight (31–45 points)

If you've been honest and scored fairly high, you're on your way. You seem to sense that if you play it safe you can spend a good part of life acting out roles and expectations rather than living joyously and freely. Whether you put it into words or not, at some level you are beginning to understand what intimacy is. Intimacy is a history of shared experiences. It is having lunch together and feeling connected even if the conversation is sluggish. It is knowing that you and your love partner share a concern about the important things. It is being at each other's side when it matters. It is seeing each other at your worst and still being there.

Those are the obvious things, the everyday things that we commit to in a marriage or long-term love partnership. And they are not to be dismissed as routine. After all, they set the tone of the relationship; it is the daily events that determine the texture of a life together. But the ways in which a relationship becomes intimate on a daily basis are only part of the picture. While the daily stability is essential, it is the easier dimension.

The part that mightily awakens fears is putting aside the mask you wear in so many aspects of your life. On the one hand it is reassuring to be able to put aside the public image and be loved for who you truly are—the darker side of your personality revealed as well—but what if you are found not lovable? It is that powerful fear of abandonment once again haunting you. All of us have such misgivings, and they are often not experienced consciously. We're aware only that our discomfort has risen and that we feel a need to get away or create distance. You may find yourself getting angry with the person who is not responding to the "real me" initially. But is it he or she that you are really angry with, or is it yourself for putting your vulnerability on the line? Can it be about not feeling accepting of yourself?

Even though you have scored high, you have not yet resolved these issues of vulnerability and self-acceptance. These are issues on a continuum from "barely" to "essentially" that challenge us all. There is no "We've arrived" when it comes to managing vulnerability and embracing ourselves, blemishes and all. There is only the journey; high scorers have put themselves on the road, but there is still a distance to go.

Using the Openness Scale with Your Partner

If you would like to use the Openness Scale to enrich your relationship, discuss each item with your partner. You don't even have to make him or her fill out the quiz. It's not about keeping or comparing scores. Instead, view the questions as a set of focused talking points.

Use the questions in any order, and don't feel you have to discuss all of them. Some people don't like responding to a question-and-answer format; they prefer a free-form discussion. Use whatever structure feels best for you.

Last, take into account the differences in the ways you and your partner respond to questions based on your background, past experiences with love relationships, and gender.

Background and Experience

Background and experience influence how willing you are to disclose feelings and personal thoughts. For example, if either you or your partner grew up in a household with a parent who was very reactive to anything that was viewed as criticism or contrary to what was deemed acceptable, you may have learned to be cautious about what you disclose. If confrontation between your parents was frequent and loud, it could be frightening to a child and may lead to an avoidance of confrontation in your present love relations for fear of re-creating the early turmoil. In contrast, if your parents adopted a "peace at any price pattern" you may have learned to do the same.

Similarly, if either you or your partner grew up in an alcoholic household, you may have learned from the instability of your past to avoid rocking the boat. The same kind of reaction may occur after a bad experience, such as having had a partner who repeatedly criticized, used your personal disclosures against you, broke your confidence by talking to others about you, or lied to you. You may be understandably cautious.

If the ghosts of past relationships are spooking your present one, you need to recognize them and take them into account.

Male-Female Differences

Men and women often differ on a number of disclosure issues. These differences come into play when men and women enter into love relationships with each other. For example, on the issue of what's private and what can be shared, women tend to be more liberal, thinking it's fine to tell a close friend about the intimate details of one's love life or a conflict. By contrast, a man may consider those disclosures a privacy violation.

Men also tend to be more reticent to communicate intimately. A man is generally more comfortable acting rather than talking about something, leading a woman to think he is withholding important information when he feels he is not. Conversely, a man may judge a woman's attitudes toward something based on what she does rather than what she says, because he is action-oriented. So he may not take what she says seriously.

Then, too, men and women have different expectations about close-ness and intimacy. A woman may be seeking more intimate sharing while a man may feel she is being too intrusive and needy. He may want more separation and space. Boundary questions like these need to be negotiated, based on each partner's expectations and needs.

Additionally, men and women may deal with resolving differences differently. Often men are less in touch with their emotions or don't want to express strong feelings because they believe emotional expres-sion isn't manly or they fear they will lose control, even become violent, if they release their emotions. But most women can handle intense feel-ings if they are expressed openly. It is withdrawal and underlying rage that disturbs them the most.

The Importance of Openness in Your Relationship

We talk about our relationships, think about them, worry about them, and ask ourselves what we really want. We say we want companionship, respect, and loyalty. But even if we have these qualities in a relationship there may be something missing. The missing ingredient goes beyond having a loyal companion to share the daily grind. Even if a love rela-tionship appears to be moving along smoothly, there may be a yearning, sometimes vague and undefined, for more.

In my research I have found that the hunger for something more in a love relationship is profound and widespread. It's there, all across the country, to be heard by anyone who will listen carefully—and I listened to more than two hundred couples. It is about sharing our inner life and thoughts with a love partner—not out of fear, not out of a need to be cared for, but out of the wish to be fully known. That is what intimacy is, the wish to know another's inner life along with the ability to share one's own. It is commonly desired and uncommonly achieved.

Far too many of us had to learn as children to hide our own feelings and needs in order to meet our parents' expectations and win their love. Adult love partnerships offer the opportunity once again to find and reveal our true self. And that is what naked intimacy is about: mustering the courage and acquiring the ability to stand figuratively naked in front of a love partner.

And what if your partner doesn't buy it? What if your partner feels, "Thanks, but I'm happy with the way things are; I'll pass on the openness"? Generally, if the desire to increase the openness in your relationship is approached in a nonthreatening, sensitive manner, you are likely to get cooperation, if not fully, at least partially. However, if your partner is resistant because of personal obstacles or is unaware of the limitations you are experiencing in the relationship, begin working for improvement by yourself. It is better to proceed yourself than to be mired in an impasse.

The way to begin is simple. Seek to be the role model of the kind of person you want your partner to become. Provide an example to follow. As a role model, you make the first move to reach out and be more open. You show more understanding and compassion when you are on the receiving end of openness.

There's no guarantee that modeling the behavior you want will produce positive results. But you have a far greater chance of getting your partner to reciprocate than if you do nothing. Think of it this way: you are creating an environment in which your partner is most likely to fulfill your needs; if nothing comes of it, at least you'll know you did your part and you will benefit by having revealed yourself.

3

OUR FAMILY LEGACY

Small children are playfully present in the world without preten-
sions or manipulations. Children possess a natural openness that is
delightfully disarming as well. However, children also possess the
strong susceptibility to being wounded if their openness is met with
judgments, rejections, or personal attacks. These wounds are
inevitably carried into adulthood.

The first world we find ourselves in, our family, is a prism through which
we view the world around us. As children we learn about openness and
intimacy based on how our parents treat us as well as on our early experiences with other family members and peers. The ideal family encourages growth and provides an emotionally safe atmosphere where its
members can be expressive and truly themselves. At their best, families
provide a secure sense of belonging, the "we" that gives us the courage
to define and develop the "I" that is unique to each of us. Having a clear
and stable sense of our self, we are more able to share ourselves with
others.

Family life is unequivocally the first and most formative school for
learning about relationships. In our families we learn not only how to

feel about ourselves but how others will respond to our feelings as well. We learn not just from what is said to us but from what our parents do directly to us and particularly from how our parents handle their own feelings and those that pass between them. In short, our family life sets the stage for relating. It is the foundation upon which we build the patterns that orchestrate love in adulthood.

But what if we have grown up in a family that was troubled? Perhaps we witnessed our parents' marriage split apart or we endured parents who stayed together and should not have. What if we grew up with a parent who was abusive or neglectful? There are so many ways that parents, though usually well intentioned, can miss the mark. Parents can be deceitful, manipulative, and untrustworthy and fall prey to all the rest of human foibles. If our upbringing was far from perfect, are we doomed to forever live in relationship hell?

Thankfully, we are not necessarily doomed. We can repair and gain an ability to have an authentic relationship with ourselves as well as with a love partner. The path of repair, although certainly not easy, and frankly not all that well traveled, awaits anyone who desires to address the unfinished emotional business of childhood. We can learn to give and receive love by transforming ourselves from unaware victims of the past into responsible individuals in the present. I know this is true, not because I studied this at a university or read about it in a book, or even because I've talked to so many people about their relationships. I know it because I've lived it.

When I was not quite five, my father died. He died suddenly; there was no time for my mother to prepare herself for the loss. Along with grief, she bore many other burdens, including unshared decisions and pressures to accept additional roles. Instantly she had to take complete responsibility not only for her children—my sister and me—but for financial records, transactions, and expenditures that my father had previously managed. A few years later, having struggled with her loss and with the pain muted, my mother married again—and again. I became a stepchild twice. Both marriages—one of seven years' duration and one of three—were ended by divorce.

After my father died, my mother was so distraught and overwhelmed by the position she found herself in—having to return to work at a time when few women worked, heading a household before the term "single parent" was in vogue, facing the world as an immigrant who had not even one year of high school education—that her children were under-parented. My sister is ten years older than I am; she was fourteen when life dramatically and abruptly was altered.

A few years later, before my mother's second marriage ended, my sister married and left home. It was fortunate for her because my stepfather was not a kind man. He was abusive. In his eyes I could not do anything right. I recall, for example, being given the "privilege" of being allowed to open the locked mailbox in the apartment house we lived in. I was unable to do it because my hand was shaking so badly in anticipation of what would happen if I didn't do it properly.

I did no better in school. In sixth grade, tests were given each week and our seats were rearranged for the rest of the week according to our grades. I vied with another boy for most weeks spent sitting in the dummy row. There was very little that I won in those days, but I succeeded at becoming the record holder. I spent more time in the last row than any of my classmates. By the time I entered high school, I was convinced I was not too bright. I was also not in danger of spilling over with self-regard. High school authorities didn't disagree. In fact, they viewed my aggressive behavior so unfavorably—and this was in Bensonhurst Brooklyn where aggressive behavior was the norm—that they asked me to leave. After two years of working at hopeless jobs, going to school at night, and managing to get myself arrested three times for unruly behavior, I left Brooklyn for college. It's not that I had any interest in college; the room and board was cheap and I had nowhere else to go.

It was at college that I met the woman who was to become my wife, and to whom, all these years later, I remain married. It hasn't been easy—especially for her! I came into the marriage thinking I was destined to be divorced eventually because I had grown up around divorce in an era when it wasn't nearly as common as it is today and when very little information was available about the impact of divorce on children. I just assumed, like mother, like son. The little that I read about divorce suggested that it ran in families. My attitude was fatalistic: "It's bound to happen, so why fight the inevitable."

In addition, I didn't feel very worthy and was forever testing my wife's regard for me by being moody, critical, and demanding. "If she sees the worst of me, will she still be there for me?" Or perhaps I unconsciously gave her the job of "fixing me" because I didn't get the nurturance I needed as a child. Or maybe I was denigrating her to reduce her power over me. It may have been all of these things. That's the nature of love: it doesn't falter on its own; we make an effort to kill it, even when we want it to live.

I didn't realize at the time that I had internalized the critical parent and was now doing to myself and to my wife what had been done to me. Of course, along with my strong offense was a hidden defense: "I can't let anyone know who I am because they'll use it against me." I had learned as a child to hide my vulnerability. After all, I had grown up with a mother who relied on me, not leaving me much room to express my own fears and concerns, and a stepfather who used anything that looked like weakness against me. It made sense that I was cautious about being too revealing.

If all that wasn't enough, I feared drawing closer and being more intimate, not only because I didn't feel worth caring about; I also believed that opening myself to love was dangerous because I had learned the pain of loss very early in life. I acted on the belief that keeping distance was protective. This way, if the relationship didn't last, I would not suffer the deep sorrow that those who have given themselves fully to love experience. I didn't give serious thought to the loss I was already experiencing—not allowing myself to bathe in the love that my wife demonstrated on a daily basis. I suppose I didn't miss it because I had never really had it in my life. It had been my experience that unhappiness came naturally; it was a familiar feeling.

The story has a happy ending. I gradually grew more aware of how my childhood had affected me. However, I spent a long time suffering at the hands of a past I had not come to terms with. Even after I thought I had stopped minimizing the effect it had on me, I continued in more sophisticated ways. I went from an attitude that the past is gone and there is nothing to be done with it to the belief that the past is still present but the impact it has is negligible. Apparently, I was reluctant to face the truth: the patterns that we have adapted in childhood are blueprints that reverberate throughout life and are especially highlighted in love relationships. There are no quick solutions; the process of becoming receptive to a deep love is lifelong. It begins with an awareness of your family legacy.

The particular form our family's influence takes varies, depending on the specific behavior patterns of a particular household combined with a child's temperament and with the role that other significant figures—peers, close relatives, teachers—play in early development. Here's a small sampling of some of the common ways early experience can manifest for adults in love relationships:

- Some people, particularly those who grew up in a family that discouraged self-expression—those who were made to feel guilty when expressing needs or feelings—become very guarded and play it safe in love relationships. They prefer to either meet their own needs or have them go unmet rather than face the possibility of criticism and rejection. Alternatively, some children who have grown up with parents who discouraged self-expression are too expressively needy later in life in an effort to make up for their earlier deprivation.

- Others that grew up in a household that did not foster realistic limits—whose parents were overly indulgent and permissive—may never learn the notion of reciprocity, and they might express feelings, especially anger, without regard to the feelings of a love partner. Their openness is raw, insensitive, and lacking in empathy, that is, without consideration of the feelings of their love partner. Their personal expressions are not really open; they are self-serving rather than facilitative of closeness.

- Still other couples, especially where both are damaged, develop a relationship based on an emotional divorce. Sometimes this evolves out of an unspoken agreement; at other times, both may agree to this openly. In either case, the relationship is empty; neither one ever reveals him- or herself, but the partners gain satisfaction from their outside activities. They may engage in frenzied entertaining, enjoy extravagant dining out, change their residence frequently, opt for elaborate decorating, and even hop from job to job. But underneath the rush of activities is the couple's attempt to fill the void left by a lack of openness and love in the relationship.

Parent/Child Relationships

Among the various people in a family, parents and siblings, the relationship with the same-sex parent is particularly important for the development of authenticity and openness. As a mentor, a mother teaches her daughter what it means to be a female, a wife, and a mother: To her mother's dismay, Alice is nearing forty and still single. Each time her live-apart lover of many years talks about marriage, she puts him off. She is still defending herself against her overbearing mother who was overinvolved with her and had no idea of appropriate boundaries. Her mother repeatedly violated her privacy in various ways, from listening in on her telephone calls to reading her personal diary. The thought of someone else invading her space, having to share the details of her life, makes her cringe and shut down.

Fathers, likewise, teach their sons the role of being male, of being a husband and a father: George is afraid to express his real hopes and feelings to his partner. No matter what reassurance his wife offers him, he maintains caution. As a child he lived with an explosive, severe father. He witnessed his father regularly berate his older brother for minor mistakes, and on several occasions he himself was the focus of his father's wrath. Those few times when, out of desperation, he turned to his father for advice, he was subjected to teasing and ridicule. Before long, George shut down and withdrew, convinced that his thoughts and feelings would bring on only disapproval.

For better or worse, children are sensitively attuned to their same-sex parent and how that parent conducts his or her relationships, especially with them and with the other parent. While same-sex relationships are important, opposite-sex parents are equally influential figures in the child's life for his or her future relationships with the opposite sex. For example, a boy whose mother is intrusive and engulfing may find himself keeping women at arm's length as an adult. A girl whose father is distant and cold may find herself either choosing a man like her father and suffering the same sense of rejection she experienced as a child or taking on her father's pattern and protectively keeping her distance from the man in her life. Both boys and girls are likely to repeat the lessons learned in childhood. The child of an alcoholic, for example, is at higher risk of marrying an alcoholic; the abused child is at higher risk of marrying an abuser or becoming an abuser.

Innumerable studies have demonstrated that how parents treat their children and how they treat each other has profound consequences for the child's emotional and social life. All the small exchanges between parent and child and between parent and parent have an emotional subtext. The repetition of these messages over the years forms the blueprint for how children will relate. Children who express their feelings and get the message that they are unacceptable or silly or irrelevant will have quite a different view of relating than children whose parents respond with respect for their feelings.

For example, if we hear from our parents that "only babies cry," we learn to suppress our feelings of distress by stoically controlling our emotions. Or we show anger to mask our underlying fears and sadness. When we are young, we may also think to ourselves, "I'll get into trouble if I cry" or "If they find out, they'll make fun of me." In contrast, if we have learned that we can manipulate our parents by phony complaints or dramatic emotional outbursts we are likely to bring these ploys into our adult love relationships. As adults we may say to ourselves something like this:

- "I'm being overly sensitive; I shouldn't feel so strongly."
- "This isn't worth getting upset about."
- "It's not worth discussing this problem. He (or she) wouldn't understand anyway."
- "If I carry on, I'll eventually get my way."

Parent/Parent Relationships

Most commonly children are exposed to their parents' chronic arguments. This is not to suggest that parents should never argue—that's completely unrealistic. However, if the arguing is chronic and dirty, it is likely children will take the attitudes that were expressed into their own relationships. Consider one example:

Sheila and Sol have been married twelve years. Sol works as a pharmacist; Sheila is a teacher. When Sol returns home he is often irritable and tired. Sheila doesn't like teaching, but she does it because they need the income. When she returns home she is equally out of sorts. To prepare himself for the unpleasant news of the day and the growing friction, Sol begins to stop for a drink after work. Sheila, disgusted with the unpredictability of his arrival home, stops preparing meals. Sol, in turn, begins eating out more frequently. They become increasingly distant and resentful. Here is a typical exchange between Sol and Sheila that their daughter, now twenty-five and in an unhappy relationship herself, reconstructed:

SHEILA: *You're late again.*

SOL: *I know; I tried my best.*

SHEILA: *Oh, bull! It's just like you to be inconsiderate. You've been drinking. You'll turn out to be a drunk—like father, like son.*

SOL: (angered) *What the hell does my father have to do with this?*

SHEILA: (angered, but controlled) *First of all, your father's a lush and you're in danger of becoming one yourself. Second, I've seen how your father treats your mother. He's late for dinner; he leaves his clothes around; he expects to be catered to. You're the same damn way, and I won't stand for it!*

SOL: (getting louder) *You don't say! My father is a controlled drinker. And who's picking up whose dirty underwear off the floor every morning?*

SHEILA: *That's a damn lie!*

SOL: *Lie, my ass! You're lazy and you know it.*

SHEILA: (sarcastic) *Sure, sure. Keep it up. And what important events occupy you all day, genius?*

SOL: *Well, I certainly don't baby-sit a bunch of brats all day, pretending to teach.*

SHEILA: (shouting) *I'm trying to get along on the money you don't make—Mr. Junior Executive.*

SOL: (walking toward the door) *Why should I knock myself out for an ungrateful bitch like you?*

It was not uncommon for the arguments that Sol and Sheila had several times a week to take place with their daughter as bystander. And it was not uncommon for one of her parents to bring her into their discord. One tactic for wreaking psychological havoc is employed by a parent who makes pointed or allusive remarks about the other parent's behavior in the presence of the children. This usually serves to embarrass and diminish the other parent in the eyes of the children. Unfortunately, it frequently works—of course at the children's expense.

Often the remarks are delivered in the heat of the battle—"Don't give me that stop-for-a-drink-and-relax crap! Why don't you just come out and say that you are avoiding me because you're such a failure!" The rationalization here is, "It is better to be honest in front of the children." But this kind of fraudulent honesty puts the children in the center of a game of "charge and countercharge." Also, under the guise of being "open and honest with the children," one parent is covertly pleading "poor little me."

Nicole, Sheila and Sol's daughter, found herself having similar negative exchanges with three of her boyfriends—the underlying themes that her parents fought over had repeated themselves in her relationships—until she recognized the pattern and began to talk more openly with her newest boyfriend about her upbringing. Not only did discussing it help to sharpen her awareness, it also furthered the intimacy between her and her boyfriend.

Caught in the Middle: Triangles

While some couples get mired in repetitive fights to which their children bear witness and some may even stop talking, other couples are even more ambitious combatants: they draw their children into their differences and form a triangle. As described in detail in my book on triangles, *Mommy or Daddy, Whose Side Am I On?*, parents create this triangle for a variety of reasons, including deflecting painful emotions in their own relationship or playing out their personal issues through their children. For example, a parent may become overinvolved with a child—being overprotective, or hoping to make the child an academic or athletic star, or in a host of other ways. This may happen because the parent is projecting his or her fears or trying to make up for his or her own lost dreams or underinvolvement in the marriage.

Unfortunately, the effects of overinvolvement with a child do not end in childhood or young adulthood; they often carry into adult love relations. For example, overprotected children often become fearful of being separate and at the same time terrified of being engulfed. On the one hand, they have learned to be frightened of being independent. On the other, they are overwhelmed by the intensity of their overinvolved parent. They become underfunctioners in response to their parents' overfunctioning. They don't have enough of an "I" sense, the sense of separateness that is necessary in order to form a healthy "we." As a result, they usually have significant difficulties with the vulnerability that comes with being open. Quite simply, they crave closeness because they fear being on their own, but they also sabotage closeness for fear of being engulfed.

Without the child realizing it, this fear of engulfment becomes a core part of adult love relations. In various ways, love is kept at bay because it is experienced as overwhelming. Such adults push others away, often without a sharp awareness of what they are doing. They keep love partners at a distance with the rationalization that they need space; some feel they are restless and free spirits at heart. The variety of obstacles at a distancer's disposal—from avoiding self-disclosure to a variety of deceptions and avoidance strategies—are endless.

Children who have an unsatisfied need for autonomy become adults who are often embarrassed by their underlying fear and lack of self-reliance. In an effort to compensate, they prefer to pass themselves off as self-reliant and have difficulty showing their needy, vulnerable, and dependent sides. They view their partner's attempts at closeness with mistrust, sabotaging or cutting off the relationship completely if it gets too intense. In short, residing within a distancer's cool exterior is a child who was not allowed to satisfy a natural need for independence.

To make matters more interesting, adults who are cautious about closeness due to the lessons learned in childhood—having had a parent that had a problem defining the boundaries between him- or herself and the child—often find that they are attracted to pursuers. Pursuers are usually people who grew up with an unsatisfied need for attachment—a parent who was underinvolved with them. They react to the fear of abandonment by seeking a high degree of togetherness and dependency in relationships. When their partner does not meet their dependency needs, they tend to pursue harder and then may coldly withdraw.

One woman, Phyllis, aged thirty-three, the manager of a large insurance agency, had particularly strong feelings about her experience:

I went through college on a scholarship and worked part time to earn extra pocket money. In my insurance agency I came in as a trainee and didn't even have my own desk. That was seven years ago, and now I run the agency! All this and my father doesn't think I'm capable of everyday kinds of things. I'm talking about things like doing the grocery shopping ("Phyllis, are you sure you have enough food in the house?") and servicing my car ("Phyllis, you know you'll ruin that new car if you don't get the oil changed"). His whole life has been wrapped up in me. And when I married the first time, in my twenties, it got worse. He didn't let up. He was always bringing food over to our place, offering to help with decorating, and giving unsolicited advice on anything and everything. He would even pull me aside for a "secret" conference to tell me Billy wasn't good enough for me—just like every guy I dated before him was never good enough. When I asked him to stop interfering, he'd get hurt and complain, "What's wrong with a father looking out for a daughter he loves?"

Billy liked my father but complained that I was too distant and guarded because, despite my bitching, I was too involved with my father. I would shoot back that our problems had nothing to do with my father. We bickered constantly. When he pulled away, I made promises to change. I pleaded, but after he relented we started the entire pattern all over again—bickering, confiding in my father, defending my actions, the whole thing. His parting words to me were that I should find someone who didn't want closeness because I was already married—to my father!

For a long time after we split I was very bitter. Now with the experience of several more failed relationships it pains me to acknowledge that he was right. It's bizarre, but I believe that our bickering was my way of creating space in the relationship. Being emotionally accessible was somehow a threat, maybe a disloyalty to my father. I wanted to be closer to Billy, but the picture of my father standing before me with that hurt look on his face didn't instill courage!

Phyllis's ex-husband, Billy, was very unhappy about the split between them, but he was not able to resolve or tolerate his wife's overly close relationship with her father. Here is how he put it:

I didn't want to leave Phyllis. I pleaded with her to look at her behavior. She never really let me know her intimately. Sometimes she even agreed with me, but it never lasted very long. Every time I came home she was on the phone. Who was it? Her father, of course! I would sit around with them and learn things that I should have known before-

hand but she saved for her conversation with her father. I felt left out and pushed her to spend more time with me. She reacted poorly to my insistence. Sometimes she would go on for days not talking to me at all. It made me crazy, I felt so rejected.

I remember her telling me when we were first going out that when she was nineteen and lost her virginity at college she called her father immediately and let him know. Now, I think that's weird. I mean if I ever have a daughter I want her to be able to talk to me, but at nineteen, shouldn't that be something that she could talk to someone her own age about? A red flag should have gone up for me when she told me that story, but I was too young and I didn't realize what the implications were. She was always relying on her father for advice about the simplest things. The slightest problem would occur and she was on the phone. He was her lifeline. I mean Phyllis would practically rely on her father to tell her when to go to the bathroom. I couldn't stand it anymore. I wanted her to be there for me. But every move I made to get us to be closer just ended up pushing her away. She would speak with her father for hours, and then I would ask for us to have some time alone. Her response was that I was smothering her. It got so I would practically say "hello," and she would say "you're crowding me." After a while I just left. How could she be really married to anyone when she was so involved with her father?

Triangulation can occur under all kinds of circumstances and in all kinds of families. In fact, sometimes, legitimate family stress, such as a child with problems, can provide the stage for triangulation to occur. Kathy Fisher, for example, described the way her son James unwittingly became a party to his parents' serious difficulties with each other.

When James was identified as slightly delayed during a routine kindergarten screening, I panicked. It was my worst nightmare come true . . . while I was pregnant I drank and smoked pot a few times. Ever since then, I'd felt guilty that somehow James would be affected. But when I told my husband about my concerns and guilt, he minimized my feelings saying I was catastrophizing the whole thing. "Children develop at different rates," he said. "James is fine; it's you who has the problem. Now you're probably going to hover over him and worry constantly so he'll think there's something really wrong with him!" "I'm not the problem, you are," I protested. "You don't worry about anything, and if he really does have a problem, you'd just ignore it and hope it goes away!"

We continued fighting like this for months, and it got even worse when I had a tutor come to work with James. He teased me about this in front of my son, and soon enough I had to battle with James to even work with the tutor. My husband had aligned himself with my son, and I competed with him for James's attention.

Before long James started to become rude, disrespectful, and cruel, not just to me but also to his teacher and other female authority figures. His schoolwork deteriorated, and he started to fight with other kids, especially girls. I blamed my husband, he blamed me, and James became more and more confused. By the end of the school year we'd been called in at least five times to meet with the teacher concerning James's academic and social problems.

Although their son's academic problem was a legitimate concern despite the Fishers' opposing views, in this case it was actually a "pseudo" issue. The real purpose of their constant fighting and discussion about James was to deflect their attention from problems they had in their relationship. During the year of fighting over their son, neither of them spoke of the lack of romantic feeling that had cast a cloud over the relationship for years. Their conflict over James successfully helped them avoid their own problems—at a price. The price was not limited to them. While the impact on James is yet to be seen, he has already begun a pattern of relating to females with hostility. This may be just the beginning.

All couples fight over these types of pseudo issues some of the time, often with great intensity. A couple going out, for example, may disagree on the directions to their destination. It begins with a simple question that barely makes the conflict radar screen—"Shouldn't you have made a left there?"—and soon they are arguing as if their very lives depended on being correct. Neither will let up, and neither will concede. Is the impassioned arguing really about the possibility of making a wrong turn?

But identifying the *real* issues is no easy matter. In a relationship that includes children it is particularly difficult to identify and work out problems. Consider these examples:

A wife says to her husband, "I don't like the way you exclude our son from your activities. I feel like he's growing up without your influence." The real issue not addressed is: "I feel neglected as well, and I am upset that you are so involved with your own activities that you spend too little time with me."

A husband says to his wife, who is considering a business promotion that involves more money and more time commitment, "I am happy that you are being offered a promotion, but the children are going to suffer and it is going to put too much stress on the household." The real issue not addressed is: "Your promotion makes me feel inferior. You'll be making more money and doing better than I'm doing."

A wife says to her husband, "You are too easygoing with the children; you are going to make it harder for them to adjust to the real world." The real issue not addressed is: "I feel as if you are the children's favorite, and I am jealous that they seem to love you more than they love me."

Childless couples can sometimes ignore their marital differences and disappointments or pretend they don't exist. They can seek compensatory gratification elsewhere, perhaps in their work or other close relationships. This is not to say that childless couples do not get sidetracked. They too bring up pseudo issues that mask the real issue. However, although hiding behind a pseudo issue will probably stunt the adult relationship, in a childless relationship it is not likely to affect other lives.

In contrast, couples that have a child or children are likely to use the children more than any other pseudo issue to divert attention from marital tension. After all, children are ever present and play such a central role in the household. In addition to being physical reminders of the marital bond, they are the only factor that cannot be excluded from the marital relationship. A couple can take a break from relatives, move away from neighbors who are troublesome, or change jobs to eliminate work difficulties. But they cannot do any of these things with their children. Even if they divorce or remarry, the children are still easy and ready targets for deflecting unresolved relationship conflicts.

The result is devastating to the children. The spoken or implied demand that they help solve their parents' serious relationship or parenting differences is an overwhelming burden having negative emotional implications that will, undoubtedly, reach far into adulthood.

Unfortunately, because of their own emotional turmoil, many parents don't realize that they are pulling their children into this destructive triangle. And those that do realize it often don't know how to stop. And through it all, the children become increasingly anxious, sad, and hostile. As adults, these children usually do not feel safe enough to be open and emotionally accessible. In fact, many of them are so confused by their childhood that they are not emotionally accessible to themselves.

Healing Childhood Wounds

It goes almost without saying that children are powerless to take charge of their lives. As adults, it is up to us, no one else, to take charge. Following are some suggestions for developing the attitude needed to get started. Note: this is not to suggest that a few simple steps will clear the way toward an intimate relationship; however, an "I can" message will get you there much faster than an "I cannot" message.

- Some people, myself included, have had the good fortune to build a happy relationship and to heal themselves through the relating. Others are not as fortunate; for those whose emotional wounds are still open, it is important to not give up. As a defense from a painful childhood, it is too easy to cut off good feelings in order to block the bad feelings. This is particularly true for men. A sense of failure and doubt may also linger from a troubled childhood for both men and women: "Is there something wrong with me, some fatal flaw that damages my love life? Can I form a close relationship? Am I capable of that?" You are, but it will take courage and persistence.

Sometimes seeking the help of a therapist can be of immeasurable assistance with your struggle.

- It is easy for a woman to come out of an angry family with a bad attitude toward men, or for a man to be hostile toward women. "No man can be trusted" or "All women want is your money" or "Men are only out for sex" are statements that serve as protective shields. What people who make these statements are really saying is, "I learned from one (or both) of my parents that it is easy to be hurt, and I am scared. Because men (women) are no good anyway, I have ample reason to be cautious." It is this attitude, usually picked up in childhood, not the basic "evilness" of men or women that prevents an openly loving relationship.

- If your home life was far less than ideal, it leaves you predisposed to self-pity. Self-pity is a damaging emotional reaction to a troubled past. It prevents living in the present or planning for a positive future. Those of us who are steeped in self-pity are more likely to repeat and reinforce former destructive patterns, see ourselves as helpless victims, and suffer from a succession of ailments and fatigue. The more energy and time we put into bemoaning the raw deal we had—this is not the same as reflecting, understanding, and working to overcome past wounds—the less energy we will have available for building a new life.

- Some people grow up with very unrealistic expectations of how other people should be. They demand a perfect world with perfect human beings—perhaps to compensate for the very imperfect world they grew up in. They become angry, frustrated, or withdrawn when things don't go their way. Because reality hardly ever measures up to their superstandards, they have a good excuse for not giving their best effort in a relationship. The failure here is to accept that we live in an imperfect world and that all the people in it are also imperfect. Disappointments are necessary for growth, change, and development. If a person is not willing to accept the fallibility of other human beings and life's inevitable challenges, the chances of finding and maintaining a close love partner are small indeed.

- Probably the most damaging family legacy is the "I am a victim of my circumstances" attitude. In contrast is a life- and relationship-affirming attitude that expresses self-responsibility: "I have the capacity to change and create fulfillment." In most areas of human interaction, there are few things that cannot be accomplished with well-directed effort. If you think, "I can't face my partner and work out our differences; I can't be honest about some things; I can't allow myself to be vulnerably open," ask yourself the following questions: If someone pointed a gun at your head and threatened to kill you if you didn't do what you say you can't do, would you do it? If your child or some other person very dear to you was in life-threatening danger and their only salvation lay in your doing what you say you can't do, would you do it? If the answer to either of these questions is yes, then ask yourself, "How is it that I won't do things for my own happiness?"

Although all families have issues, they may not be that obvious. To reflect on your upbringing, it sometimes helps to talk with a close friend who spent a lot of time in your home or to have a discussion with your siblings. What were your outstanding memories? Were they positive or negative? What do you notice about the patterns you have formed in your adult relationships? Are some of your patterns productive and satisfying while others are not? Are any of these patterns familiar as you reflect back on your family of origin? Relationships lose their vitality without openness, and openness is obstructed not because we are mindless or weak but because our perspectives are too limited and our strengths misdirected. One of the most rewarding things you can do is to sit down with your partner and discuss your view of how your upbringing has affected your relationship. If you have one, bring your family photo album to the discussion and use it as a prompt for your memory as well as a discussion jumping-off point.

Some people have particularly provocative family histories, including alcoholism, physical abuse, and sexual-boundary violations. This is likely to make it very difficult to be emotionally available and manage the vulnerability that comes with real intimacy. If this is true for you and you question your ability to fully reveal yourself, or you are uncomfortable with a partner who is self-disclosing, seeking the assistance of a therapist is a wise move.

4

GETTING PERSONAL

FEELING TALK

As people become more open with their feelings, an evolution occurs. Gradually, they realize that there's less need to guard against issues that were previously viewed as threatening; for instead of hiding from feelings, the open person welcomes them— their own as well as those of others.

Love's capacity to make us happy is rivaled only by its capacity to make us miserable. One thing is certain: happy or miserable, or somewhere in between, there is no relationship that men and women experience that is as provocative, sought after, and confusing as romantic love. Love may make the world go round, but the spin often leaves us dizzy. That is especially the case if we are not familiar with the language of love. It is like being in a foreign country and not being able to communicate. It is actually worse, because in a foreign country you are usually accorded the courtesy of being a foreigner, and expectations are scaled down accordingly. In the country of love, the expectation is that you know the language.

In love relationships, feelings are the voice of the heart. Certainly the intellect plays a significant role in love, but it is the heart that speaks most powerfully. When feelings speak, we are compelled to listen and sometimes act, even if we do not always understand why. As Henry Roth wrote in his classic novel *Call It Sleep* about the power of speaking from the heart, "If you could put words to what you felt, it was yours." The corollary, of course, is that not being aware of your feelings or not knowing how to use or express them is a handicap, particularly in a love relationship.

Arguably, feelings are the core of love relationships. A love relationship does not center on sharing the rent or household chores or even coparenting; it is distinguished by emotional involvement. So much of what really matters in love depends upon our feelings. Consequently, to be awash in confusing or dimly perceived feelings is overwhelming. The problem is that there are many forces that combine to make awareness and expression of feelings something other than a simple matter.

Sure, when you are drowning in feeling, what you are experiencing is hard to ignore; the grand passions, for better or worse, are grabbers. But life is made up of experiences that aren't dramatic. Everyday feelings are mushy, difficult to discern, nonpalpable, slippery things. They are easy to misread or overlook. It starts in childhood, when many of us learn to hide or mistrust our feelings. Here are some sample exchanges. They come from a Mommy and Me group I visited a number of years ago:

CHILD: *Mommy, I'm hungry.*

MOMMY: *You can't be. You just ate.*

CHILD: (louder) *But I'm hungry.*

MOMMY: *You're not hungry. You're just a little grumpy. Let's play a game.*

CHILD: (wailing) *No, I'm hungry!*

* * *

CHILD: *Mommy, it's hot in here.*

MOMMY: *It's chilly. Keep your sweater on.*

CHILD: *But I'm hot.*
MOMMY: *It is not hot. Keep your sweater on!*
CHILD: *No, I'm hot.*

*   *   *

CHILD: *I don't like this game. It's boring.*
MOMMY: *No it isn't. It's very interesting.*
CHILD: *It's stupid.*
MOMMY: *It's fun and you can learn from it.*
CHILD: *It stinks and I don't like it.*
MOMMY: *Yes you do.*

At such moments, children learn deep lessons. One obvious conclusion from these exchanges might well be that your mother doesn't care about your feelings. Suppose you were the child who was hungry, hot, or bored? And suppose you wanted that all-important grown-up in your life to know what you were feeling? However, instead of understanding you, the grown-up was telling you repeatedly not to trust your own perceptions but to rely on hers. After a time it is likely you would be careful about expressing your feelings for fear of being wrong. And if you can't be free to feel what you feel openly, you're in bondage regardless of the freedom of the society you live in.

One of the moms in the group, Stephanie, was the friend who had invited me. After the meeting she asked what I thought, and I told her—not harshly, but directly and without cushioning. For an awkward moment there was a strained silence between us. Then she said, "You know, I think you're absolutely right. I'm going to work on it."

Three weeks later we met for lunch. It was progress report time. "What I did," Stephanie said, "was put myself in my children's shoes and tune into what they were experiencing. When I did, it didn't feel like I was using some technique; it felt natural. I even felt closer to my kids. I would say things like, 'I like this game, but I can see that you don't care for it. You find it boring.' It wasn't that difficult at all, and the kids responded real well. Then one day my daughter announced that she didn't like her friend Jennifer's mother—who just happens to be my best friend. 'Jennifer's mommy is mean and no fun. I don't want to see her anymore,' is what she said. It didn't take me long to respond. 'That's a terrible thing to say,' I reflexively snapped. 'It is mean to talk that way about Jennifer's mom. I don't want you talking that way about anyone, especially someone as nice as Jennifer's mom!'"

That exchange taught Stephanie something else about herself. She could be very accepting about most of the feelings her daughter had, but if her daughter said something emotionally provocative, Stephanie would regress to being defensive and shutting out her daughter's feelings. Stephanie's reaction isn't all that unusual. In fact, it is common. Very few adults can recount a childhood where their feelings, especially those that provoked their parents, were accepted. Although we are all different and are capable of having different feelings without being right or wrong, it is rare that parents are able to recognize and validate our feelings. That is the beginning; it is the point when we start to disown our feelings, especially those that we have been taught are unacceptable. And with that we lose a part of ourselves. We also divert our energy. It takes energy to block an emotion, and it takes energy to free one.

Later, when we go to school, we learn about math, geography, and grammar, but feelings are rarely part of the curriculum. As adults, we are busy: we have goals to reach and achievements to attain, and days pass quickly without much attention to feelings. Your job may be shaky, one of your children may be sick, and you may have a cold coming on, but if a casual friend asks in passing how you feel, you will probably reply, "I'm fine." This kind of superficial exchange is merely a sign of friendliness, not an expression of feelings. Life is full of such rituals, of harmless small talk. The trouble is that over the years these shallow, habitual responses become so ingrained that they combine with our childhood experiences and make it easier to devalue the importance of feelings.

Consider this: you are at work and you have completed a big project that you are anticipating feedback on. You worked your heart out on the project, giving it your very best effort, and you secretly suspect that the project manager is going to shower you with accolades. In fact, you are hoping that the success of your efforts will propel your career to a new level. After lunch you are called into the manager's office.

The anointing hour has arrived. The first thing you notice is the glum look on the manager's face. Although he is never upbeat, he looks more dour than usual. The meeting goes from bad to worse in a hurry. You are devastated. Your manager's final words to you are that he expects a better effort next time, and when you start to reply he puts his hand up and asserts, "I am not in the mood for excuses. This meeting is over. . . ."

As soon as you arrive home you spill the whole story to your partner. Your partner does not respond supportively. You nod but don't say anything, secretly vowing not to expose yourself again. Or perhaps you storm off.

Not dealing with feelings comes with a steep price. As the maxim goes, if you don't deal with your feelings, your feelings will deal with you. A lifetime of inattentiveness to feelings is strikingly demonstrated by Paul, an accountant, and Marla, his wife of twenty years. Two months before this conversation, Marla had asked Paul for a separation:

PAUL: *I've never felt able to be open with you about the things that really bothered me, the most personal things.*

MARLA: *I realize that. I felt the same way about being open with you. But I've pushed myself and encouraged you to do the same. I'm lonely with you. I wanted to be more passionate with you, less reserved; but I always felt you didn't really want that.*

PAUL: (stunned) *But, Marla, I never knew that. Why didn't you tell me how you felt? Why didn't you say something?*

MARLA: *I am not into becoming one of those women who are constantly ragging on their husbands. I've told you how I felt and you didn't respond. After a few rounds of that I just stopped. I thought that was the way you wanted things. Why didn't you ever say anything?*

PAUL: (crying) *For the same reasons, I suppose. I took it for granted that you were happy with the status quo. I just didn't get it. God, I wish I had listened more carefully back then, Marla!*

The waste of time, energy, and potential happiness through the years of Marla and Paul's marriage, when what they both *really* wanted was so much more similar than what they each *supposed* the other wanted, is appalling. Yet this same kind of waste characterizes millions of relationships.

Hidden Feelings

The point has been repeatedly made: connecting on an intimate basis requires that both people in a relationship reveal themselves in a personal manner. Too often, though, an opposite process occurs. Held back by fear and influenced by conventional social discourse, we use language that masks our personal reactions. For instance, we refer to important events in remote "it" language:

SHE: *I feel very much alone, separate from you. I don't like my feeling.*

HE: *What should we do about it?*

In the man's response to this woman's statement, the feeling has become an impersonal "it," and the tense has been changed to the future. The risk now is that the conversation will move too quickly to planning future ways of correcting the situation without exploring the feeling involved. A more personal response to her pain, which includes a measure of immediacy, would be simply, "How do I contribute to your aloneness?"

Using "it" is often appropriate in business situations. Indeed, most places of employment reward the worker for his or her ability to focus exclusively on "it": the product to be sold, the work to be done. Personal reaction is restricted to a note in the suggestion box, a comment to a coworker, or perhaps an airing in a special brainstorming or gripe meeting under controlled guidance.

In marked contrast, personal conversation emphasizes what is going on inside a person, because the object is to become known. Here, elements that are quite commonplace in professional or casual conversation are either unnecessary or potentially damaging. In this regard, statements beginning with "it" externalize responsibility; the listener finds it difficult to respond because the speaker has not accepted ownership of what he or she has said. For instance, in the statement, "It is difficult talking to you," "it" is out there somewhere, part of neither the speaker nor the listener. A sentence that communicates more intimately is "I have difficulty talking to you."

"It" statements are underresponsible because they leave ownership of the feeling or thought in question. "We," "everybody," and "all" statements are overresponsible because they pass ownership to everyone (and therefore to no one in particular) and so tend to diffuse experience: "*Everybody* else liked the movie"; "*Most* people would be angry about this"; "There are *those* that believe in capital punishment"; "*We* need to budget more conservatively." In these statements, neither party feels or thinks something; it is the nebulous "we" or "them" that is being referred to, and responsibility is being diluted. "We need to budget more conservatively" may be restated with ownership as, "I am concerned about our finances, and I want you to spend less money."

In addition to whitewashing a personal reaction, overresponsible statements are often used to provoke an individual to feel guilty or incompetent. The disguised intent of "Everybody else liked the movie," for example, might be, "Because you are in the minority, there must be something wrong with you."

Still another means of diluting responsibility for our thoughts and feelings comes in the form of qualifiers and disclaimers: "If you don't mind me saying so . . ."; "I might be wrong, but . . . "; "I know you're sensitive; however, . . ."; "This might sound silly, but . . ."; "Although you probably disagree, . . ." The disclaimer can also be a phrase tacked on after a slightly challenging remark: "It was an awful evening—wasn't it?"; "We should rearrange our priorities—I think"; "I'll go along with your judgment—I guess." Each disclaimer apologizes for the speaker's temerity in daring to offer an opinion. The disclaimer also gives the listener "permission" to disagree.

Stripping away qualifiers and disclaimers brings force and vitality back into a statement. Contrary to most formal education, which urges a modesty many of us do not possess, qualifiers obscure and drain the personal element from a conversation.

His Marriage and Hers

As if all the factors already discussed weren't enough to make the all-important focus on feelings and personal statements complicated, there are the differences with how men and women interact to consider as well. The conventional wisdom suggests that women want a closer, more personal relationship and men resist it. Women complain that the man in their life is focused on business, sports, and things rather than feelings; they say he is not being open about his inner life or particularly interested in hers.

Consider a couple, Joseph and Sarah, both in their midthirties, as a case in point. They began, as so often occurs, with a whirlwind courtship. Here is Sarah's accounting of their relationship:

> Our meeting was absolutely beautiful and very romantic. Joseph was a blind date arranged through a mutual friend. I don't ordinarily make blind dates, but my friend really urged me on this one. She was right! We went to dinner but never noticed the food. We couldn't talk enough; we got misty-eyed again and again; we were so enraptured with each other. Joseph and I went back to his apartment and talked and made love almost all night. I had had plenty of relationships that were mostly sexual, but I knew this one was different, and so did Joseph. After six months, when he asked me to marry him, I wasn't surprised—it was natural and inevitable.
>
> The beginning of our marriage continued in the direction of our courtship; we both shared a sense of warmth, a feeling of being loved, a feeling of having taken out an option on a partnership. We considered ourselves to be best friends and shared our deepest feelings. This

kind of sharing and disclosure made us feel very close. We told things to each other that we'd never confided to anyone else. Sometimes we'd lie in bed and talk into the small hours of morning. Our whole inner world seemed to spread out for us to explore together. But as open and emotional as we were in the early days of our relationship, just so shut and frozen did we become over the years. Now we have so little to say. Little by little we have bottled up our feelings—both of love and of resentment—until we seem to feel nothing at all for each other.

The vitality seems to have been sapped from our marriage. Our sense of each other, the openness, had been superb when we met; over the years it faded and shrank until our original ecstasy was no longer recognizable. We were simply too busy—he with his career, I with the responsibilities of our home and family—to notice that we were no longer intimate. We no longer shared our private lives. Our feelings were not part of our lives together. Joe would retreat as soon as he came home—to the garage where he worked on restoring an antique car or into the den where he built ship models. On those occasions when he was receptive or cheerful, I was resentful of all the times he wasn't and, spitefully, did not make myself available. In return, when I took an initiative to talk openly, he would demonstrate his disinterest by promptly falling asleep. After a while, conversation just about dried up; we went from total openness to a closed, guarded marriage. The only topics we discuss now are the weather, the children's clothing, and gossip about other people.

The ironic thing about this is that my friends who knew us when we were enthusiastic about our relationship would always rib us about our nonstop talking. They would comment that going out with us felt like an intrusion—we were so taken by our own conversation, and talking about our feelings about this or that, that they hated to interrupt. That seems like a very long time ago; now we are together for the simple reason that we cannot endure the thought of living alone. I have cultivated a kind of existential resignation and wry humor about the whole thing. "Don't take it all so hard," I tell myself. "All marriages are like this!" But in all honesty, I don't really believe that. There must be more to it. All the women's magazines from Red-

book *to* Cosmopolitan *always give the same advice: stroke him, massage his ego, tell him what he wants to hear, and he'll open up. Pretend. That's such a bunch of nonsense. How can I have a "repair" conversation based on dishonesty and deceit? It is difficult enough to be agonized by the void in our relationship. I am not about to add lies and deception to our comedy of errors. The problem is, at this stage of our relationship, how can I express my true feelings and needs in a way that is not threatening or seen as blaming. Lately, I have felt that the real barrier between us—the cause of our lost intimacy—is not really about filling the air with words, but the lack of feeling talk between us. We have become strangers to each other's experience of life. What happened? Was it that we started the relationship at breakneck speed? Was it the kids, the work pressures, or that Joseph was simply dead inside?*

Sarah eventually left Joseph. Once again, the conventional explanation of what happened is that Joseph simply did not want the closeness that Sarah desired and eventually their relationship just dried up. However, there's another explanation: their breakup did not begin with their whirlwind courtship or the stress of bringing children into their lives and the pressures of earning a living, nor did it emanate from Joseph's lack of desire for closeness. It began in childhood with the differences between the emotional worlds of girls and boys.

The deterioration of Sarah and Joseph's marriage is not unique. There are, in effect, two emotional realities in most couples: his and hers. Most researchers concede that boys and girls are brought up in divergent ways, taught different skills, rewarded for diverse acts. Witness some discriminating reactions to male and female children: a shy little girl is considered cute; a shy boy is thought of as a sissy. A frightened girl is comforted; a boy is admonished to act like a man. Girls are allowed comfortably to kiss each other and to cry openly without shame; boys who even touch each other had better be "horsing around," and crying is done only at the expense of ridicule. Boys enjoy less time on a parent's lap, even if they have hurt themselves; girls are encouraged to share their feelings, especially if hurt.

It is apparent that boys and girls are taught very different lessons about handling emotions, and this divergence is telling in the early relationships they form. As I reported in my book *Friendship,* boys tend to form play groups that are competitive in nature; girls' groups more frequently revolve around cooperative enterprises. Thus, at an early age, boys become concerned with trying hard and winning while girls, by contrast, play house and school, engaging in roles that require complementary support and bonding. If a girl becomes hurt or upset during play, the other girls gather around her and comfort her; if a boy is hurt or upset, he is expected to get out of the way while the game continues.

From Hercules to James Bond, the heroic man is presented as impenetrable. This suggests the possibility that the stoic, Clint Eastwood–type of male imperturbability may represent a defense against feeling emotionally vulnerable. Men are drawn to these types of heroes because unconsciously they represent a fantasy that is compelling. It is the wish to avoid feeling out of control, to avoid that anxious, shaky experience—the kind of experience that many of us felt the first time we had to speak in front of a group: exposed, naked, weak, and helpless. As one man aptly put it, "Having to bare my soul reminds me of having to give a speech in my English class. As I was walking to the front of my class I felt defenseless, like a lamb led to slaughter."

The capacity of men to manage feelings has come under research scrutiny, and the findings are quite revealing. Consider this finding: Robert Levenson at the University of California at Berkeley studied more than 150 couples, all in long-lasting marriages, and concluded that husbands uniformly found it significantly more unpleasant and even aversive to become upset in the face of disagreement. In fact, wives did not mind entering into emotional territory with their husbands; they were the initiators.

Another researcher, John Gottman, a psychologist at the University of Washington, sheds further light on the male propensity to avoid emotional interaction, especially if it is, or threatens to become, intense. He found that men experience emotional flooding at lower levels than women do. That is, men become emotionally overwhelmed—they feel swamped. From a physiological perspective, when this happens, men secrete more adrenaline into their bloodstream and take longer to recover from this than do women. Interestingly, if they withdraw, Gottman's research demonstrates, their heart rates drop by about ten beats per minute, giving them a sense of relief that reinforces this behavior. Adding to the mix, however, is the finding that when men withdraw, women's heart rates increase!

Quite possibly, one of the reasons men avoid emotional contact is that they are not sure where it is going to lead and want to avoid feeling flooded. The dance that follows comprises a man moving backward while his female partner advances, stepping up the emotional volume. Each is attempting to position him- or herself more comfortably. Instead, they solidify a distancer/pursuer pattern that leads them down the unhappy road that Sarah and Joseph followed.

It comes down to this: by way of varying social conditioning and quite likely differing biological wiring, men and women deal with their emotional lives in a manner that creates frustration and anguish. As if it is a cruel trick, the onset of the conflict does not occur during the ecstasy of the honeymoon period, but afterward, when commitment has been made and their hearts have become entwined. If relationships are going to succeed on an emotional level, men are going to have to stretch, because by way of socialization and biology, they are not naturally suited for feelings being the basis of their interactions. Women must also stretch, primarily by not taking the difference in this important aspect of their relationship personally. It is not about them; it is about the different ways men and women interact. That is the point: it is not that men don't want closeness; they simply approach it differently.

While there are differences between the sexes that widen the gulf between men and women on the plane of openness and self-disclosure, there is also a side to this that both sexes experience. As one man said to me, "Real openness is taking off the mask that we wear in our daily lives." Taking off the mask is an exciting prospect; at some level all of us want to be accepted for who we truly are, not some facade that we have learned to put on to fit others' visions. The most satisfying relationships by all accounts are those where we can show our darker side—

those hidden and less acceptable feelings—without fear of reprisal. Most of us hunger to be accepted for who we are, without pretense.

When we are with someone with whom we feel emotionally safe, it is not only relaxing, it is rejuvenating. It is as if we have been injected with a feel-good drug. Of course, the other side of this experience—the side that discourages both men and women—is the risk involved. The question comes up, sometimes not quite consciously: Is the *real* me lovable? What if I let it all hang out and I am rejected? That's a frightening prospect for anyone, male or female. It suggests that we are all shaky about how lovable we are, and being found undesirable is a gruesome experience that is reminiscent of a child's fear of abandonment. And the fear of abandonment, of being found undesirable, appears to be equally distributed between men and women.

Countering the Tendency to Neglect Feelings

A very powerful method for countering the tendency to talk around feelings rather than directly to the feelings is empathic listening. To understand thoroughly another person's thoughts and feelings and to be understood thoroughly by this person in return are among the most rewarding of human experiences and, unfortunately, all too rare. In the examples that follow, we will see how a couple interacts ineffectively and how the same issues can be discussed more sensitively.

Judy and Jerry have been married for eight years. They have two children, ages five and six. Jerry is an executive in a large electronics firm. He has a good job, and they live very comfortably. Jerry drives home from work on a summer evening and is greeted at the door by an exuberant Judy.

JUDY: *Hi, sweetheart. I've got great news.*

JERRY: *Terrific. What's up?*

JUDY: *I could hardly wait until tonight to tell you. Remember how I've mentioned my boredom and feelings of uselessness in the past? Well, today I did something about them. I went over to the college, filled out an application form, and had an interview for the nursing program. I was told my chances for acceptance are very good, and it is likely that I'll be starting in September. I'm so excited.*

JERRY: (angrily) *What about the kids? What about your responsibilities here? How the hell can you start school with all that? Nothing doing! We don't need extra expenses and more chaos!*

JUDY: (angrily and defensively) *Who the hell do you think you are? You can't live my life for me. I'm bored, I want something meaningful to do, and I'm going back to school.*

JERRY: *Oh, no, you aren't!*

JUDY: *Oh, yes, I am!*

JERRY: *I won't let you. I'm not going to give you the money.*

JUDY: *That won't stop me. You bastard! I'll borrow the money. I'm tired of being a bored, depressed, and burdened housewife. No one's going to stop me from taking care of myself.*

JERRY: *Is that all you think you are, a housewife?*

JUDY: *No, I'm much more. I'm a baby-sitter, cook, window washer, waxer, cleaner, and clerk—and I've had it. I start school next month, and that's all there is to it.*

JERRY: *You can't.*

JUDY: *I can and I am. That's final.*

JERRY: *You're not, and that's final.*

Here's a replay of this couple's conversation, this time with each acknowledging and respecting the other's feelings.

JUDY: *Hi, sweetheart. I've got great news.*

JERRY: *You really seem excited. What's up?*

JUDY: *I am excited. I could hardly wait until tonight to tell you. Today I finally did something to counter the boredom and sense of uselessness I've been experiencing. I went over to the college, filled out the application form, and had an interview for the nursing program. I was told my chances for acceptance are very good, and it is likely that I'll be starting in September.*

JERRY: *Gee, you really seem high about this. I wish I could share your enthusiasm about going back to school, but I have mixed feelings about it.*

JUDY: *Mixed feelings? I don't understand. Why are your feelings mixed?*

JERRY: *I'm not sure. It's so sudden. I haven't had a chance to think about it . . . on the one hand, I'm glad you're enthused about something. I know you've been in the dumps for a while. But there's something frightening to me about this. I also feel funny that something as important to you as going back to school wasn't discussed with me until now.*

JUDY: *It sounds as if you are really thrown by this. It really is kind of sudden. I've been thinking about it for a few days, and when I decided to do it, I wanted to surprise you. It seems I shocked you instead.*

JERRY: *You did. That's for sure. There are lots of things that scare me about this.*

JUDY: *For example?*

JERRY: *What about the kids? Are they going to be shortchanged?*

JUDY: *Well, both of them are going to be in school in the fall. I met with a counselor today and planned a tentative course schedule that doesn't conflict with their after-school hours. I'll be able to make it home substantially before them in the afternoon.*

JERRY: *Boy, you've really planned this thing out. It must mean a great deal to you.*

JUDY: *It does. It is vitally important to me. And so are you and the children. But I recognize that I have been restless and out of sorts for a long time now. I have been inattentive to myself and my own needs. I've been bored. There is no challenge in my life.*

JERRY: *You aren't satisfied with the loving feelings we all have for you?*

JUDY: *I am, Jerry. But it isn't enough. We all have strong feelings for you. Would you be satisfied being a "housefather"?*

JERRY: *Come on now. You know that wouldn't be enough for me.*

JUDY: *I feel the same way. It's not that these other things aren't important, but I miss the stimulation of the world outside this house.*

JERRY: *I have to say this, Judy, I'm also worried that you'll be less available to me when you start school.*

JUDY: *It's true that I'll probably be busier and have less time for you, Jerry. But I'll have a renewed zest for life. I think this will be communicated to you and the children. I believe I can be a better person and, consequently, a better mother and wife by not ignoring my own development.*

JERRY: *You present a pretty convincing case, Judy, but I can't say that I'm totally comfortable with the idea. I appreciate how important this venture is to you, and I respect your right to pursue it. I realize that if I were in your place, I would do the same thing.*

Judy: I understand that this will be a transition for you as well as for me, Jerry, and there may be some difficulties that will have to be worked out. But I'm confident things will fall into place.

In this couple's first conversation, they quickly became adversaries. Their dialogue was primarily authoritarian and judgmental ("We don't need extra expenses and more chaos!"), threatening and counterthreatening ("I'm not going to give you the money"; "No one's going to stop me . . ."). This kind of dialogue rarely produces a resolution of the issue at hand, and both parties are likely to storm off bitter and resentful. The all-too-familiar result of this kind of exchange—which may be yelled, signaled by angry glances, or telegraphed by hurt silence—is: "Everything would have worked out fine if you hadn't upset me" or "You just don't give a damn about my feelings." Developing openness and resolving important personal issues satisfactorily requires recognition of and respect for a partner's feelings and point of view. These qualities were conspicuously lacking in the first dialogue.

In the replay dialogue, although Judy and Jerry were not in total agreement about the issue ("I can't say that I'm totally comfortable with the idea"), they communicated an understanding of each other's position and feelings ("It must mean a great deal to you" and "This will be a transition for you as well as for me, Jerry"). It was as if they were silently asking, "How does he (she) see it? How does he (she) feel? How would I feel if this were said to me?" This is empathy, a critical ingredient in mutually satisfying relationships. It is an effort to understand another's beliefs, practices, and feelings without necessarily sharing or agreeing with them. When the individuals in the dispute realize they are being understood, that someone sees how the situation seems to them, the statements are likely to grow less exaggerated and defensive, and it is no longer necessary to maintain the attitude, "I am 100 percent right, and you are 100 percent wrong."

While empathy does not require agreement with the other's view, it does preclude the demand that, "You must think, feel, and act like me." Empathic relating is actually a radical departure from usual forms of relating. Many of us are unaware of the tremendous pressure we put on our family members to have the same feelings we do. It is often as though we silently say, "If you want me to love you, then you must have the same feelings I do. If I feel your behavior is bad, you must feel so too. If I feel a certain goal is desirable, you must feel so as well."

Empathy is made up of two main components. One is listening and attempting to understand another's view rather than busily preparing a rebuttal; the second is communicating this understanding to the speaker.

An experience that frequently helps to develop this pattern of communicating is role reversal. With role reversal, when a discussion involving differences in personal/emotional issues occurs, it becomes the responsibility of each party to state the partner's position and feelings until she or he is satisfied with the degree of understanding achieved. If she or he is not satisfied, a brief "time-out" is called while that person's position and related feelings are expressed again. The discussion does not proceed until each partner is satisfied that the salient aspects of his or her position are understood. Consider this example:

HIM: *I'm out there all day long, getting one turndown after another. Being a salesman is tough. Some days it really gets to me.*

HER: *Cooking and cleaning—that's my day. What the hell are you complaining about?*

HIM: *Hold it. Time out! You passed right over my feelings. Can you please restate what I said from my viewpoint?* [He is asking for an empathic response.]

HER: *It sounded as if you were trying to make me feel guilty, and I won't have any of that.* [Rather than looking at his feelings, she is still focusing on her own.]

HIM: *That wasn't my intention. I was just feeling a bit frustrated. Do you understand?* [He is restating his position and asking her to express *his* position in her own words.]

HER: *I understand now. You are feeling frustrated after a day of rejection. It's just that I had a lousy day also.*

HIM: *Sounds like you are also pretty frustrated. What's the matter?*

If a couple conscientiously practice this, though it may seem forced and silly at the beginning, many difficulties not caused by actual differences but by misunderstandings and emotional alienation will be prevented. What's more, when feelings are identified and expressed in an empathic manner, a couple will sometimes find that the real difficulty has little to do with what they are arguing about. An argument about flirting at social gatherings, for instance, might be only a symptom of two people's assumptions: "If you loved me, you wouldn't do this" or "If you respected me, you'd trust me." The fears behind the assumption are quite similar: "I'm afraid you don't love/respect me." At this level, seeming differences turn in to shared experiences; that is, each partner might feel emotionally threatened by the flirting or the command to stop, and the surface disagreement might be only an expression of the differences in the way each partner avoids or copes with very similar feelings and experiences. Only by being sensitive to each other's feelings will a couple achieve a level of discussion where these discoveries occur.

Keeping the Heart in Love: Additional Advice

We all get emotionally bogged down from time to time. Being emotionally bogged down is a condition of imbalance in which feelings are trapped instead of expressed. Keeping feelings from being expressed employs defenses and drains energy. The more feelings are held back, the less energy you have to be yourself and the less you have to offer a love relationship. What's more, if you're emotionally bogged down, your feelings will eventually "leak" out in the wrong direction, or your defenses will become so rigid that the love in your life will starve from lack of emotional nourishment.

Here are some suggestions to avoid getting emotionally bogged down and to enhance the love and affection you have. First, let's consider some general comments for both relationship partners and then some remarks specific to men and to women.

- Most of us have had the childhood (and adult) experience of being told that what we are feeling is somehow not OK. Make a concerted effort to allow yourself to feel whatever you feel without making a value judgment. Remind yourself that your feelings matter. That means that if you feel something, you need to muster the courage to express it. Expressing feelings can certainly be unsettling, especially if you are not accustomed to doing so, but holding back puts another brick in the wall between you and your love partner. If you use up your energy trying to convince your partner that you are not hurt, afraid, or angry when in fact you are, your relationship will deteriorate rather than grow.

- No matter how discouraging your past has been or how restricting your upbringing, there is plenty of basis for a rich love life if you can learn to accept your feelings. To be open, you need to understand what you feel, know where that feeling comes from, and be able to express that feeling. If you get stuck ask yourself: What am I afraid of losing? How may I be hurt? Am I afraid of accepting some part of myself? As you ask these questions of yourself you will find, over time, that you can answer them more easily. You will become more aware of your feelings and get through the impasse. If you exercise muscles they become toned and respond more effectively; in similar fashion, if your feelings begin to be acknowledged and expressed more freely, they, too, will respond naturally. In those instances when you are unable to identify your feelings at the moment when you are discussing something with your partner, continue to think about it after your discussion. If you come up with afterthoughts, share them with your partner—later is better than never. It goes something like this, "Remember yesterday when we were talking about . . ."

- Men need to avoid sidestepping emotional content in their interactions with others, especially their love partners. For example, when your partner brings up something that is feeling based, rather than symbolically rolling your eyes, "Here we go again," consider it an act of love. It is an attempt to keep the relationship healthy and vital. If feelings are presented strongly, rather than viewing them as "hysterical," "over the top," "premenstrual," or in some other negative manner, consider them to be a demonstration of the passion your partner has about the issue being discussed.

- Just as it is important for men to stay with their partner's more feeling-laden expression, it is equally important for them to bring their own feelings into their interactions. I was witness to a couple having a conversation about a flight the man had just taken overseas. He was describing a series of problems the plane had experienced. "We took off," he said. "Then there were engine problems so we had to make an emergency landing. We took off again, and there were more problems so we landed again. Would you believe it happened a third time? Then things went smoothly." The man's partner sat in stunned silence until she finally blurted, "Oh my goodness, how did you feel? I would have been in a panic!" The man had described the experience with the objectivity of a journalist reporting the news. He was not comfortable sharing his anxiety, nor does this man bring his feelings into conversation. For men, it is essential to ask yourself, "How do I feel about what has happened?" and to bring those feelings into the discussion.

- Men also need to be wary of short-circuiting a discussion with their partners by offering practical advice prematurely—unless it is requested. It is usually more important for women to feel heard and understood. Women often regard a solution early in a discussion as an indication of impatience or dismissal of her feelings. Most important, women want to feel (as do men, when they think about it) that their feelings are acknowledged and valid.

- As for women, bear in mind that men are socialized differently. Because men are usually put off by strong emotional outbursts, especially if they are critical and directed at them, it is important to make a purposeful effort to tone it down. This is not to suggest clamping down on your feelings, but rather to calm down, at least somewhat, before dealing with a hot issue. Think of it as writing—most writers do not want to go public with their first draft. The second (or third) draft doesn't lose anything; in fact it is more thought out and effective. If you have strong feelings and express them without any reservation whatsoever, it will almost certainly lead to your partner stonewalling or becoming defensive, neither of which will leave you satisfied. In addition, if you are finding you are losing the attention of the man in your life when you give him all of the details of an emotional issue, try being more succinct. You know how he surfs through the channels, giving each one a split second? You don't want to be one of those channels that gets passed by. Although all of the details are important to you, he is likely to be more encouraged to listen if you get to the point more quickly.

Just as it takes some energy to block or hold back your feelings, it also takes energy to express your feelings. The journey begins the same way for all of us, male or female, by deciding to attend to our feelings and asking ourselves with as much honesty as we can muster: What do I feel? Where is that feeling coming from? What event is linked to it? Talk about your reflection with your partner, even if it isn't fully formulated. With practice, you will be in touch with a new source of intimacy between you and your partner.

5

CHALLENGING YOUR VULNERABILITY

All of us have a vulnerable side, just as all of us have strength and competence to draw on. When we cannot express both sides with some balance, then we are not operating with a whole and authentic self.

Vulnerable literally means "able to be wounded." In common usage, we refer to being vulnerable when we're feeling fragile and emotionally penetrable. In medical parlance, the word is often used when a patient's immune system is compromised and he or she is particularly susceptible to illness. The way most of us think about being vulnerable is that it is not a pleasant experience, and it is to be avoided if at all possible. The association is to weakness rather than to strength.

Indeed, appearing or being vulnerable does have drawbacks in many aspects of life. Men and women employed as police officers, airline pilots, lawyers, and teachers, as well as those employed in a host of other occupational categories, are required to appear in control. Even if they feel vulnerable, they are encouraged to present themselves with a superficial facade that belies this. In fact, ask any man, regardless of his occupation, if he would volunteer to feel and appear vulnerable, and he is likely to opt for a root canal instead. Women may be socialized to accept vulnerability more readily, but it is not an experience they relish.

From the first time our feelings are hurt as children, we begin to struggle with the issue of vulnerability. How much of ourselves do we expose, how much of ourselves do we suppress in order to be loved? Although we don't have the words for it, we observe our parents to see how they handle feeling vulnerable. If our parents are guarded and closed, they serve as role models for exercising emotional caution. The old adage, "Don't show too much of yourself because they will use it against you," becomes part of our unwritten life rules. In contrast, if our parents are open and bold in exposing who they are and how they feel about things, we are likely to enter the world with refreshing courage. However, even if our childhood experience has been positive, an adult love relationship presents a challenge. For it is in this experience, a love relationship, where the potential for feeling vulnerable is greatest.

There are innumerable ways to feel vulnerable—when you are frightened of losing the love and respect of your partner, when you've done something that turned out badly, when you're afraid that someone will discover your limitations—and we've all suffered through some of them. In an effort to stay on top of the situation, it's common to turn the tables and go on the offensive. Rather than face the feeling of vulnerability, some people withdraw, others become critical of someone else or hide the feeling of vulnerability behind humor or laughter, and still others take on an air of superiority. Even our facial expressions are affected by our fear of appearing vulnerable. Many of us are masters of the cocktail party grin, the passive gaze, the social smile, and the cool stare—all the shields used in everyday life to guard against being emotionally transparent.

Vulnerability in its most basic form is the experience of feeling exposed. That is why it is especially likely to be provoked by love—the most personally challenging relationship any of us will ever have. Consequently, in love relationships, many of us proceed with caution—particularly after the "high" of the courtship period has subsided. Vulnerability, especially with those closest to us, is often perceived to be dangerous and frightening. Communicating in an intimate manner can be terrifying because it places us in the precarious position of being susceptible to rejection or humiliation on a deep level. This is an experience most of us fear and those of us who have had it would like never to experience again.

The possibility of being rejected or in some way ridiculed when we have exposed ourselves is so unpleasant that we fear it, even if the evidence of past experiences with our partner suggests we are safe. It is like the fear of taking a flight in an airplane. Despite the high likelihood that the flight will be safe, even the remote possibility of a disastrous outcome can cause the jitters.

Here are a couple of illustrations. The first is from a man who has been married for twelve years. He and his wife began with the feeling of openness that many couples experience and that most find hard to sustain:

> *I don't know how to explain it, but I just can't get myself to feel relaxed with Sharon the way I felt—at least most of the time—when we were dating. Now it goes something like this: Sharon comes into the TV room, and I am sitting there watching some stupid program. I'm not really even watching; I'm just staring at the TV. This is my way of avoiding my feelings when I am not in a good place emotionally. She looks at me and asks what's wrong. Interesting—she can read me without me saying a word. My wife is asking me what is going on; she cares. The sensible thing would be to tell her that I'm feeling lousy, that my knee hurts, and that I'm worried about how things are going at work. But I don't react sensibly. I say, "Nothing, I'm fine." She gives it another try, "You sure? What's up?" Once again, I give her the non-response response. This time it's a mumble, "Nothing. Nothing's up. I'm just watching a program." Then she goes for broke. "It doesn't sound like nothing's up and everything's fine. You seem upset about something. Talk to me!"*
>
> *You would think I would let it out, but I don't give an inch! Something holds me back, and I don't even know what it is. There's just something that I can't get past. And as if that wasn't confusing enough,*

there is also a part of me that doesn't want her to stop! How crazy is that? I feel annoyed that she's bugging me, but I don't want her to stop. Yet when she does take an interest I feel I have to circle the wagons. And this is the little dance that we do, probably a couple of times a month, at least.

This man isn't alone in his ambivalence about feeling vulnerable. It is difficult for all of us to come out of our comfort zone, to leave the emotional status quo to which we've become accustomed. Depending on the extent that we protect ourselves, we may experience a sense of safety but simultaneously feel alone and isolated. It is not surprising that couples learn, usually over a period of years—after the "infatuation drug" of the courtship period has worn off—to eliminate conversation that touches on areas of sensitivity and conflict. They may feel unsafe with each other emotionally—perhaps they have used each other's disclosures against one another. Neither may have developed a capacity for revealing him- or herself, or one of them may simply be worn down from the effort to expand the other's tolerance for vulnerability in an effort to create more openness. Whatever the basis for the impasse in the relationship, sometimes they do it so well that relatively little remains for them to talk about.

Here is the commentary of the wife of the man we just heard from:

Bob is just so frustrating to me. The last thing I want is to be a nag. I don't need to know every detail of his life. I don't have time for every detail! And I don't bore him with the minutiae of my own life. But it is the real stuff that goes on with him that I want to know about. I want him to be able to tell me when something is not right, when he's worried about something, when something is bothering him. Damn, I want to be his friend! Instead, he zones out in front of the TV and becomes impenetrable. You would think that I am looking for something to use against him. I'm not. I never have. I just want him to take the chance to open up to me, to let his guard down with me. As it is, we have become great at small talk; we are so good because we are so practiced at it. But isn't that supposed to be for casual relationships, not for the person you are sleeping with? How weird is that?

How does she cope with her husband's response to her? What stops her from being more open with her husband, despite his guarded response to her? These are the questions I asked. Her answer surprised me; she brought up something about the issue of vulnerability that I was not expecting.

> *I cope by relying on my friends. I know I'll probably never get from Bob what I get from my closest girlfriends. And, if I am to be honest about it, because I've thought a lot about this, there is a part of me that is secretly not too unhappy with the way things are. I am frustrated when I run into Bob's wall, but then again I am not obligated to expose myself to him. That's not how the relationship is organized. Maybe I don't have the courage to have that kind of relationship with him—revealing myself and being vulnerable with him. With my friends it's different. I don't sleep with them; I am not as vulnerable with them. It's just different.*
>
> *Somehow, I can say things to my friends because I don't see them all the time. I don't have to face them the next day. If they see "the real me" and reject me, I will be very upset. But that's not the same as it would be with Bob. We've been together for nearly twenty years. If he rejected me—not out of his own avoidance issues but because he saw me completely exposed and he didn't like who I was—that would be devastating. It is different between my friends and my husband. And I am not convinced it is because they are women. I know it is pretty strange, but when I am really honest with myself I realize there is something about that wall he builds around himself that is actually reassuring to me. It's safe!*

Imagined Danger?

What is it that this woman needs to feel safe from? Why does our vulnerability index rise in relation to our love partner and fall in relation to those with whom we have a less central relationship?

The operative word is *central*. Whether a couple is getting along or not, whether they are open with each or not, in a committed relationship our lives revolve around each other. Even those who are newly separated by their own choice will acknowledge that there is a part of them that feels empty without the other person—the person they asked to leave! The irony is that, for better or for worse, in time our love partners become increasingly a part of the fabric of our lives. They are part of our daily experience; it is with them that we share the everyday events, even if they are limited to the mundane. After some time, they become the "constant," the part of our life that becomes familiar, even if it is a discordant familiar or we take them for granted; it is oddly comforting because it is predictable. The more important a love partner becomes, the higher the stakes become and the more of a risk we experience in losing that person's validation of our feelings and views, especially on sensitive matters.

It is not only deeply personal and sensitive issues that become provocative. In love relationships, even small issues can take on disproportionate sensitivity. In long-term relationships it is very easy to become dependent on your partner's view of you. You want your partner to see you the way you want to be seen or understood. You do impression management. The result may be frequent bickering that makes little sense to an outsider but takes on a life of its own for the couple involved. Regardless of the specific content, it reduces to: "I am not!" and "You are so!" The point of the bickering, of course, is to "correct" your partner's view so that he or she is in accord with your own views. The origin of these dynamics begins with our upbringing.

We all start out being the smallest, least powerful person in our immediate world, the family. We need our parents to survive. It is important to please our primary caretaker, usually our mother, to get the things we need. Our life literally depends on doing so. It is appropriate in childhood to look to others, to be dependent on their love, sympathy, and understanding. As children we look to ourselves only secondarily. As adults it is our challenge to grow beyond needing another person to approve of us in order to feel secure. However, it is much easier stated than carried out.

Approval is very powerful, particularly the approval of the person with whom you have chosen to spend your life. Even the thought of possibly being found undesirable summons up fears of abandonment, if not consciously then at an unconscious level. That is a "leftover" from childhood that is difficult to overcome. To be abandoned is a terrifying prospect for a child. A child couldn't survive it. In reality, for an adult aloneness is something quite different. Adults are not harmed by disapproval, but to reveal yourself and be found wanting is a terrifying prospect nonetheless.

It is testimony to the power of a love relationship that it can, even for those who appear to be emotionally sturdy, bring back the echo of childhood ghosts. There is nothing like a love relationship to regress us to a childhood state of powerlessness; it is the closest we will ever come to the sensitivity and reactivity we had to our parents as children. Childhood was a time in our life when the words of our parents echoed in our heads and influenced us greatly. This is not to suggest that we always heeded their advice—we may have even rebelled against it—but their words mattered. For many of us, that is the experience we have with a love partner in adulthood.

You can mix with people all day and feel on top of it, and then you come home, and a single word or even a look throws you off. At times it feels like being a grown-up child. Nearly everyone in love has said or, even if it hasn't actually been verbalized, has realized that no one in their life can get to them in the enormous way their partner can.

Sometimes the childhood experience of feeling weak and powerless that most of us fear is not altogether hidden and subtle; it bubbles to the surface forcefully. Here is how Frank, a writer married for eight years, described his experience:

I made a big mistake with my wife. We were sitting around talking about another couple. Then my wife asked if she could confide something about the woman in the other couple, who happened to be a close friend of hers. I said, "sure," having no idea what could be so personal that I would have to be sworn to secrecy beforehand. She told me the other woman was having an affair with another woman. Well, I became very judgmental, and we got into a huge argument. One thing led to another, and in the heat of things my wife blurted that she too had had a "fling" with another woman, just before we were married. I freaked out, and she ran into the bedroom crying and screaming. She packed a bag and left the house. At first, still steaming, I didn't realize the impact of her leaving. The anger I felt—not so much about her revelation but about the fight we had about it—protected me from the gravity of what had just happened. She left!

That night when I woke up and looked at the empty space in the bed next to me, I had a full-blown anxiety attack. I remembered that as a child I had a congenital lung impairment repaired; my mother left me in the hospital in a private room in the winter. This picture came to me of the huge hospital building—the gray, dreary room—and it got dark every night very early, between four and five o'clock, when the shadows came across my bed, and my mother would put on her coat and say, "Good-bye," and I wouldn't see her again until the next day.

And one day she didn't show up. She had an accident that evening and was hospitalized herself. In the confusion, no one told me. She just wasn't there. That feeling of panic and abandonment is what came back in spades when I stared at the empty space in the bed next to me. I was that little boy again—confused, frightened, feeling helpless and very, very vulnerable.

This man's experience illustrates the power of loss. Loss and its "cousin," the fear of abandonment, are the underbelly of our struggle with allowing ourselves to tolerate feeling vulnerable. When we think of loss, we think of the loss through death. But loss is a far more encompassing theme in our life. For we lose not only through death but also by being left, by the fear that our true selves will be found wanting and we will lose love. This was the experience of Harold, married fourteen years. After having bared his soul to his wife during a period when he was drinking to excess, he talked about his regret that she had seen a side of him that he was ashamed of:

There are times, when I am driving or sitting at my desk, and it comes to me. I know my wife is going to leave me. She'll either fall in love with someone else or just fall out of love with me and move on. I feel a sense of despair about this. I showed her a side of myself, a weak side of myself that I manage to keep hidden when I am sober, and I just can't imagine her still loving me after that. Whenever I see her walking out the door, I feel as if she is never coming back. She reassures me, but I don't feel more secure. I think she is doing it only because she feels pity for me, and I don't want her pity.

My temptation is to cling, or to become angry when I think about her leaving, and it takes all my energy to fight against this. I don't want to act like some weepy sap and bring on just what I fear. But I feel so exposed. And it is not that I told her some real deep, dark secret. I didn't because I don't really have one, other than the fact that I really don't feel good enough to be loved. My parents were both very critical people, the kind of people that you can never please, and it has left me cautious about telling too much of myself. One thing is for sure: I am not drinking any more, and I am not letting her see the weaker side of me, no matter what. I've done enough damage.

Sometimes to avoid feeling exposed and vulnerable we put on an act to keep from being known. Justifying the act is the belief, unconscious or implicit, that to be one's real self is dangerous, that exposure of real feelings will somehow lead to being found undesirable. This kind of belief has some basis in reality. We let our hair down with a love partner only to be told we are not behaving in a manner that is satisfactory. We go to a meeting and speak openly only to receive disapproving looks—often from others who had the same thoughts but dared not give them voice! From early childhood our parents encourage us to be our authentic selves, yet at the same time they give us another message—fit their vision of who they think we should be. They (and our love partners) often want us to be a certain way for their own needs. While it is frightening to really expose yourself, playing it safe is not as safe as it seems. Whether people conceal themselves and their vulnerability behind banter, name-dropping, business talk, abrasiveness, humor, appeasement, or any one of a number of false fronts, the result is the same. All facades are cover-ups for the fear of being vulnerable to hurt.

Hence they defeat the possibility of an open and authentically nurturing love relationship.

It is only natural to want to protect one's well-being. However, "wearing a disguise" does the opposite; it reduces us by inhibiting intimacy and resulting in self-alienation. The path of challenging and stretching our tolerance for experiencing vulnerability is paved by our willingness to forgo our usual efforts to control things, to manage others'—especially our lover's—impressions of us. If we are stuck in false behavior as an ongoing pattern, we may go through the motions of love but essentially we remain unrevealed and hence unconnected.

Creating Balance

Is the answer to set limits on the degree of openness in your love relationship, to play it safe and maintain a comfortable status quo? Or is the answer simply to let it all hang out and wear your heart on your sleeve? It's not a simple "all or none" consideration. Vulnerability, like many factors in relationships, is not without its complications. Too much vulnerability and you are likely to burst into tears if your love partner so much as brushes your sleeve without saying excuse me.

In its most destructive form, vulnerability produces self-pity, self-doubt, blame, and an effort to close off emotional experience. For example, Diane, a fifty-one-year-old executive, suffered a devastating loss of confidence when she was abruptly given notice that she was being removed from her position and replaced by a (younger) woman she had trained. She put on thirty-five pounds, doubted her judgment, dropped out of the job market altogether, and secluded herself. Here's what she said:

> *I thought I was doing a great job. How could I hope to be right about anything? I simply lost control. I felt as if I had regressed to being a helpless, powerless child. I had no control over my feelings. The only way I was able to feel better, at least temporarily, was to comfort myself with food. And I needed a lot of comforting. I ate and I shopped. Then I returned what I bought. I couldn't even decide what*

I really wanted and what was simply my indulgence. It got so that the simplest decision stumped me. I'm talking about whether to have butter or jam on my toast, that sort of thing. I wasn't really depressed. My mood wasn't depressed. I was sleeping well. I was sad, for certain. I was definitely angry. But the biggest problem was that I just felt so weakened, like someone snuck into my head and stole my database for being a grown-up. The rug was pulled from beneath me. My emotions were raw. I had given my heart to my job. And now I just felt like my heart was irreparably broken. I was only about an inch away from screaming, "I want my Mommy!"

That's vulnerability at its worst. Yet, without vulnerability, intimate relating and life itself is devoid of meaning. The capacity to suffer along with a loved one as well as to be open to your own pain and disappointment is a crucial component of a healthy relationship. After all, vulnerability at its most basic is simply an indication of your ability to be affected by things. The only invulnerable people in our lives are dead. No one alive is invulnerable. And if they are, they haven't found love. Love requires a degree of vulnerability. It's a matter of balance.

Although vulnerability definitely involves exposure and risk, it is also an opportunity for deeper self-awareness; it enables us to see and understand things we ignore when everything in a relationship is going smoothly. For one woman, in a live-in relationship with a man for the past two years, the vulnerability produced by an accident led to a shake-up:

I was crossing a street, and I was hit by a car careening around a corner. My leg was broken very badly, and the prognosis for walking normally again was guarded. Basically, my lover simply disappeared. I was frightened to death. All my life I was a very physical person. I had run marathons, for God's sake. Sam listened, but he responded in a way that just didn't feel authentic. It was like he didn't want to have to deal with it. He told me he wasn't good in dealing with disability, I told him I wasn't good in dealing with a good-time lover, and we split.

One thing I learned goes back to needing a real partner, not simply a playmate. It's not because I want someone to take care of me. The experience I had convinced me I could take care of myself. I can't imagine that being open about myself, letting someone know who I am, including parts of me that I am not thrilled with, can be more harrowing than the dramatic physical change I endured after the accident. I need someone with courage because I want to live my life with someone who will face me as well as himself without facades. If I am to have a real relationship, I need someone with the courage to be real! I need someone who is not afraid of feeling vulnerable. For that I need a grown-up.

Vulnerability. Without it, our relationships are sterile; with too much, emotion runs rampant, making closeness impossible. Whether we like it or not, developing a deep connection with a love partner requires being open and emotionally available, and that involves vulnerability. It may take courage, but there is a payoff: when we do meet heart-to-heart and emotionally naked, the experience is exhilarating, unlike anything we encounter in other aspects of our lives. Perhaps the most reliable way to feel connected is for you and your partner to allow yourselves to be known by being open about feelings and thoughts. Revealing ourselves—our failings as well as our successes, our quirks and our interests, our likes and dislikes, our less than endearing qualities as well as our strong, likable ones—is conducive to an open and deep love relationship.

When your partner lets you know what he or she genuinely thinks and feels, and when your questions about him or her are answered truthfully and without reserve, this inspires openness. While you may not always like what you hear, knowing where you stand in relation to a love partner is usually preferable to being left guessing. Secretive or closed people may present themselves as an interesting challenge, but with the passing of time, not knowing what they feel or think about significant personal issues creates distance. Essentially, a negative cycle begins where one or both partners limit the personal character of the relationship until nothing vital remains.

In sharp contrast, as we explore the stirrings of openness with a love partner, we are likely to feel better about taking the risk to further expose our vulnerability. As our risk-taking bears fruit, we feel progressively more confident to further open ourselves and reveal our true feelings, communicate our private thoughts and values, and be ourselves. In short, the more openness that develops, the safer we feel to take further risks in the direction of being fully seen, leading to an enrichment of the love relationship.

Although being self-disclosing is important—for we cannot establish true closeness if we do not permit ourselves to be known—most of us find it a difficult process. We've learned to guard our vulnerability as a result of past hurts, real or imagined. Hidden behind our caution is often the belief, conscious or implicit, that to be one's real self is dangerous, that exposure of feelings and thoughts will lead to being unwanted. It comes down to that oft-repeated phrase: "If people found out what I was really like, they wouldn't want any part of me." Make no mistake about it: abandonment is the most primitive and terrifying of all human fears. The common experience of wanting approval, avoiding rejection, and being successful all touch on being seen as desirable—insurance, we hope, against abandonment. One woman described how her fear affected her love life. The very first thing she told me about herself was that her father had died when she was a child:

I was six years old when it happened. My father went on a business trip, and he never returned. He had a heart attack and died in his hotel room. I barely have memories of him, and my mother didn't help the situation. She fell apart, and it was as if she had left as well. As an adult, the relationships that I have had have been turbulent. Sometimes I play it safe and cautious by not revealing too much of myself. Other times I get very involved and very intense. There have been times in the first week of a relationship that I am saying, "I love you," wanting to be with the man every minute and talking about being together forever. As soon as the man pulls away slightly, I begin accusing him of wanting to leave. Typically, I find someone else and leave first. Then I enter the new relationship feeling burned and take an opposite approach, cautious to the point of feeling like I am an undercover agent trying to avoid discovery.

When I'm alone, I feel empty but more relaxed. I realized recently that when I'm alone I don't have to perform; this accounts for the reduction in tension. Over the years I have developed a knack for determining what kind of woman a guy likes and then playing the role. Even if this pleases the guy, it creates a tension within me; because they have an inaccurate concept of me, I am left with the burden of maintaining the pretense.

Sometimes I even surprise myself by taking positions that I don't really feel if I think that would please a guy I want to impress. It's been so long since I stood up for my convictions that I don't know what I feel or what my beliefs really are. I haven't been honest with myself. "Be yourself," I hear people say. It sounds easy but it's not. I don't know what my real self is; I've lost touch with that.

This woman is talking very honestly about her fear of being left once again in her life. While many of us have not been traumatized by an early loss, we are still very sensitive to being found wanting. It is easy to fall into a pattern where our life is guided by what we think we should be or by the expectations of others rather than by who we are. It rarely works.

Frequently, when a love partner relates in a limited or contrived manner, it influences us to wonder what he or she really feels or thinks. Consequently, we tend to be wary and cautious, uncertainty leaves us feeling insecure, and we are not quite sure where we stand in the relationship. In contrast to guardedness, open interpersonal behavior in the long run feels secure; it promotes intimacy.

To pick an easily recognized example, consider a small child who has not been compromised by a limiting environment. If the child expresses affection or anger or contentment or fear, there is no doubt in our minds that he or she *is* the experience, all the way through. The child is transparently fearful, or loving, or angry; there is no deception, no pretense. Perhaps that genuineness is why so many people respond warmly to small children—we know exactly where we stand with them.

Of course, by the time most of us have reached adulthood, many complicating factors have entered and contaminated the process of self-disclosure. For one thing, many middle-aged adults today grew up in a household in which openness between their parents was not even an aspired goal. Deceptions and lies are almost institutionalized—standard operating procedures between the sexes. As a result, rather than sharing the closeness of a love relationship, many women and men live in their very separate emotional worlds.

While vulnerability usually promotes intimacy, some people, more often women, go over the top with it. To them, Mr. Right is that special someone who will reveal a magical depth of spiritual communion in the form of intense discussions about his deepest feelings. Unfortunately, this idyllic picture of the soul mate is very hard for some women to give up; consequently, they are forever being "betrayed."

And while some women complain that they want more openness, they may not always be receptive when it occurs. One man had this to say:

I am overweight and have been my whole life. My father was overweight, my mother was overweight, and my sister is overweight. If there is a fat gene, we have it! I've tried every diet on the planet; I've lost weight dozens of times and eventually gained it back. It has been an enormous struggle. As I've gotten older I've started to experience the health problems that eventually come with being fat. I am now diabetic and my joints ache. I realize that years of stressing my joints have worn them down. When I share the problems I am having, my wife tells me how it is my entire fault. She gets angry, and it isn't as if my aches and pains are the only things I speak about. Her attitude really bothers me. After all, I was fat when I met her, and she knew that this was something that I wasn't successful at overcoming. Finally I said to her, "I see you don't want to deal with the problems I'm having because of my weight. I'm not going to tell you anything anymore." Her reaction was even more confusing. She was insulted that I didn't want to talk to her about anything anymore.

And then one day we were talking and she admitted that she couldn't handle it. She really didn't want to hear about my struggle. She really didn't want to know. She told me she just wanted to hear that everything was just great and that I wasn't deteriorating. Otherwise, she said, she felt insecure, and that made her angry. She told me this as a kind of confession, and I appreciated her honesty, but where does that leave me? Whom do I talk to?

Good question—should this man persist or perhaps keep his health problems to himself? Can being too open erode a love relationship? And what factors should be considered before broaching sensitive issues?

As a general rule, honesty and disclosure is the best policy for promoting intimacy. However, there are such factors as timing, interest of the other person, appropriateness, and the effect of the disclosures on either participant that must be considered in any such judgment. Most of us, especially men, are not in danger of being too open. The problem is being too protective, not permitting enough vulnerability.

My experience with couples is that avoiding issues starts off innocently enough, but over the years withholding increases and accumulates until there is very little left to discuss. It is as if a couple is on an island and each decision to avoid a subject erodes the ground between them until there is barely enough to support them. In the previous example, the woman in question would be wise to discuss her insecurity and anger rather than avoid the discussion simply because it creates discomfort. Some things don't go well together: if a man or woman is looking to stay in a comfort zone, a vibrant love relationship is not in the cards.

The Power of Vulnerability

Vulnerability, as we have seen, has many faces. Allowing yourself to be vulnerably open to your love partner's full range of felt experience requires courage. Being courageous means taking the chance of revealing yourself and being open to your partner's disclosures even though you are unsure and frightened of the consequences. Moving forward into more openness while acknowledging your anxiety rather than attempting to avoid or discourage it is the path of growth. Yes, you may jeopardize the safe (although devitalized) relationship you have; you are putting yourself on the line. You may feel embarrassed, and you may be judged.

It is apparent that we all want to feel cherished for who we are without having to resort to pretensions or manipulations, especially in a love relationship. The bind we are in is that we can also be rejected for who we are. Being ourselves and boldly stepping out into the world means letting go of control over how our lover may feel about us.

Of course, in reality, we have no control over anyone's reactions to our unguarded inner selves or whether they will give us the acceptance, respect, and love we want. Taking the risk of being truly open may expose you to being rejected or judged harshly. Some individuals who are frightened of their own inner being may prefer us to be cautious, indirect, or restrained. Unsettled by our honesty and directness, they may reject us. Others, however, who are more in touch with who they are and are without pretense or facade, may resent our propensity to hide feelings, withhold the truth, or manipulate in order to gain approval. In such instances we may be rejected not because people dislike who we are but because we are not allowing ourselves to be fully who we really are. It is a matter of the type of relationship you want, both with yourself and with the person with whom you have chosen to share your life.

If you choose to develop the emotional muscle required to tolerate the feeling of vulnerability, you will find that you will become more accepting of yourself and of others. In time you will find yourself becoming even more willing to be open, and it is more likely that you will get the sensitive response that meets your need for real intimacy.

Following are some suggestions for tolerating vulnerability and staying emotionally open, even under difficult circumstances:

- Own your own issues. For example, Lisa was convinced that her husband was hopelessly insensitive and that all their marital problems resulted from his selfishness. She missed no opportunity to tell him just that. After a painful separation followed by considerable reflection, she began to own her side of the problem. Never having experienced a father who was emotionally available, she had wanted her husband to be the "good parent" she never had—one who was continuously and selflessly attentive to her needs. Of course, he could never fulfill such fantasies and eventually became involved with another woman as an escape from the confusion and discouragement he felt in his marriage. For a time, Lisa self-righteously blamed her husband for the marital difficulties. It wasn't until she openly discussed her part in their conflicts that their differences were effectively reconciled.

- Rather than tightening the grip on your feelings, let go. Many of us fear losing control. However, if you give expression to your feelings and resist the temptation to be defensive, you are less likely to lose control. Getting angry or crying, for example, is not being out of control; it is merely expressing intense feelings. In fact, the very fear of losing control usually results in denying feelings—feelings that build up to trigger arguments and explosions.

- Keep a small notebook with you each day for a full week. Jot down each and every evasion, no matter how petty (for example, complimenting someone falsely, smiling when you're actually annoyed, telling people what they want to hear). Study the notebook at the end of each day to determine patterns of inauthenticity. Share these deceptions with your spouse, and make a commitment to gradually change your behavior, to be more open, more vulnerable.

- Stop judging your partner. Focus on expressing how you feel rather than on the nearly impossible task of trying to change your partner's behavior. By doing this, you are drastically shifting the usual nagging scenario and offering an invitation to your partner to respond sensitively, because he or she is less likely to feel attacked. By simply sharing how you feel in response to your partner's words or actions without pressure or threat, you open an opportunity for him or her to voluntarily respond in an accommodating manner. Indeed, for people who care about one another, self-revealing communication can be very compelling. In fact, some studies suggest that when a person permits him- or herself to be vulnerable, empathy is an innate human response.

- Although using self-revealing statements to sensitively share your feelings may appear to reduce you to a weaker position in terms of getting what you want from your relationship, in reality the opposite is true. On the surface, it may seem that fighting for change is the stronger and more effective strategy. However, there is a hidden power in vulnerability—it does not equal weakness. In fact, a special kind of inner strength is summoned when asserting genuine feelings rather than blaming, attacking, moralizing, and using other types of manipulation. Even if your partner is not responsive, you are more likely to respect the integrity of your expression. In contrast, angry, accusatory growls typically camouflage a host of unacknowledged fears or unexplored areas within yourself that you have yet to understand, or accept.

- If your partner just bought you an expensive anniversary gift that you didn't like, what would you do? You might be afraid of hurting his or her feelings and "fake" it, acting as if you liked what was bought. Rather than do what is conventional, consider these types of awkward situations differently. Take it as an opportunity to show your vulnerability. You might explain that you are very moved by the thought and gesture, but although the gift was given in love, it is not something you will put to good use. What's more, if you are feeling a bit uneasy and anxious in disclosing this to your partner, tell him or her that as well. Many of us have these feelings in awkward situations—do we handle it forthrightly or do we fake it? Often the first reaction is to fake it. However, especially in your love relationship, try being open. Being open and allow-ing yourself to experience feeling vulnerable doesn't mean being perfect or polished in your honesty. It means showing yourself, blemishes and all.

Following these guidelines will assist in providing the strength and courage to love well—to muster the courage to be vulnerable without feeling overwhelmed.

6

SECRETS

THE GOOD, THE BAD, AND THE VERY BAD

Secret keeping involves self-deception because we focus on its protective functions rather than its limiting aspects. Indeed, keeping secrets is especially problematic in love relationships because we feel closest to the person with whom we are sharing our secrets and uncomfortable around anyone from whom we are withholding.

Secrets come in all sizes, degrees of complexity, and forms. We are told something by a friend and asked to keep it a secret—even from our partner; we have certain things about ourselves that we won't tell anybody, especially those closest to us; and we have opinions regarding those closest to us that we don't share. Secrets abound between parents and children. Some of these secrets reflect healthy boundaries; other secrets between the generations are problematic. The disclosure of some secrets is often dramatic and seared into memory. Other times, the secret itself is not nearly as powerful as the deception and energy it takes to maintain the secret.

Secrets are often seen as necessary and protective. We may withhold something about ourselves because we believe that revealing it will deem us as unlovable or that if we are forthright it will harm another person; consequently, we convince ourselves we are being protective. For some, hiding information or feelings from others provides a sense of independence and power. For others, it is an attempt to ward off unwanted attention or intrusion. Secrets often serve as a way to avoid having to deal with issues that we are unwilling to confront. While knowledge is power, some people view secrets as supercharged power, using them manipulatively to barter and leverage.

Indeed, secrets are an integral part of our lives. According to a poll of one thousand married people published in *Reader's Digest* (Lague 2001), more than three quarters have kept secrets from their spouses. It is no wonder. We are brought up surrounded by secrets. They have their beginning in our family of origin. Parents keep secrets from their children to maintain privacy and to shield them from disclosures they are not emotionally prepared for. Children conceal information from their parents to avoid punishment or disapproval, to protect a parent from worry, and to foster a sense of separateness.

As stated earlier, some family secrets are in the service of healthy functioning, but often that is not the case. What begins as something innocent often spreads like an infection involving more lying, silence, guardedness, suspicion, and denial. If honesty serves to bring people closer, secretiveness often leads to estrangement.

Secrets are not only a part of all of our families, they are central to our culture. If you've ever watched a soap opera, noticed the underlying drama in several hit movies or bestselling novels, or seen a Greek tragedy, you know that the family secret is at the heart of many story lines. For better or worse, secrets have infiltrated our daily interactions. Secrets fascinate us.

Out of one closely guarded secret—the unknown "love child," the illicit affair, the hidden suicide, the double life, the undisclosed previous marriage, the history of being molested, or the criminal past—writers spin hundreds of hours of gripping drama. Secrets change with the times. A half-century ago, for example, divorce was kept secret; coming from a "broken home" was a basis for shame and derision. Currently, divorce is so common, and so publicized, particularly among those who have attained newsworthy status, that it's shock and shame value has been defused.

Issues like adoption, alcoholism, homosexuality, and depression have also been significantly disarmed of the emotional impact they once had. Consequently, they are not, for the most part, as closely guarded as they had been in the past. In fact, it is now the darkness around them that packs more punch than the actual secret.

There are many ways in which secrets burden the secret holder, but usually secrets touch on one aspect of emotion that we all strive to avoid: shame. We attempt to keep secret what we are ashamed of, and we become ashamed of what our family and culture has taught us is shameful. In his masterpiece of writing on shame, *The Scarlet Letter*, Nathaniel Hawthorne depicts the sense of personal agony of having a secret exposed. Hester Prynne is a woman who is an acknowledged adulteress. As her punishment, she must wear the scarlet letter *A* so that her behavior is made public. Here is a passage from Hawthorne's work zeroing in on the experience that we try to avoid with secrets:

> *She grew to have a dread of children; for they had imbibed from their parents a vague idea of something horrible in this dreary woman . . . first allowing her to pass, they pursued her at a distance with shrill cries, and the utterance of a word that has no distinct purport to their own minds, but was none the less terrible to her, as proceeding from lips that babbled it unconsciously. It seemed to argue so wide a diffusion of her shame, that all nature knew of it; it could have caused her no deeper pang, had the leaves of the trees whispered the dark story among themselves—had the summer breeze murmured about it—had the wintry blast shrieked it aloud! Another peculiar torture was felt in the gaze of a new eye. When strangers looked curiously at the scarlet letter—and none ever failed to do so—they branded it afresh into Hester's soul; so that, oftentimes, she could scarcely refrain, yet always did refrain, from covering the symbol with her hand. From first to last, in short, Hester Prynne had always had this dreadful agony in*

feeling a human eye upon the token; the spot never grew callous; it
seemed, on the contrary, to grow more sensitive with daily torture.

Shame inevitably involves exposure and includes anticipation of disgrace. In the case of Hester Prynne, it is public disgrace that she was sentenced to do by the Puritan tribunal. Shame is a very powerful factor behind secret keeping because we are socialized to be conscious of appearances and to focus on "how it will look" or "what others will think" rather than on more substantive measures of self-regard.

Most of us learn a sense of shame from our parents and other influential adults in our early life. The circumstances that surround shame are often shrouded in secrecy and vary from incidents that are easy to identify with to those we shrug off as not worth the cover-up. In short, one person's secret is another's yawn.

Here is an illustration of a woman whose secret began over an issue that would seem to be minor; for her, though, it was consuming. Dolores is in her late thirties, and she grew up in a household that was very guarded. The talk around her dinner table was about things, not people and not feelings. If ever there was discussion of personal issues, it was about the foolishness of neighbors or friends who revealed too much of themselves.

Dolores was married to a man with close ties to his family. She secretly resented the attention he lavished on his siblings, his parents, his aunts, and his uncles to the exclusion of her. She was ashamed that she felt the way she did because she herself was raised to believe that family loyalty was essential and that her role was to bring happiness to her husband. Her anguish over her feelings was exacerbated in that her husband worked in his family's business, and each evening he came home and talked of his day with his siblings and parents. She listened while her resentfulness simmered and built up inside her. Each night she considered talking to her husband, and each night she talked herself out of it. "He is a good man," she told herself. "He works hard, and his family members have done so much for us. How could I interfere with his relationships? They make him so happy; I am just being selfish!"

One evening while her husband was working late, Dolores went to the local mall to do some shopping. She was in one of the large stores when her heart began to palpitate, her breathing became rapid and shallow, and she felt as if she were going to faint. Dolores dropped the merchandise she had been considering, ran to her car, and rushed home. She was having what was later described as an anxiety attack. At first she thought she was just tired, or perhaps she hadn't eaten enough, but when the attacks became more frequent she consulted with her family physician who referred her to a psychiatrist. The psychiatrist prescribed medication, but she did not want to take the medication. For a time she coped by staying close to home and making sure that she ate properly and slept sufficiently. Despite her efforts, her ability to function became increasingly limited and required her husband to be with her more and pay closer attention to her.

Initially, her husband responded to her requests with consideration, but as time passed and her condition was worsening, his patience was wearing thin. One night, after her husband witnessed her in the middle of an anxiety attack, he became so upset that he insisted she consult with a psychologist. When she refused, he threatened to leave her if she didn't do something to get better. He insisted he could not keep up with a reduced work schedule and "hold her hand" indefinitely.

After her initial consult, the psychologist requested that she bring her husband to the next meeting. "Why?" she asked defensively. "It is my problem. What does my husband have to do with it?" "When you are able to talk to your husband about the feelings you are hiding from him, your anxiety will start improving," the psychologist suggested, having quickly realized that her symptom was speaking for her. In effect, her symptom was saying to her husband: "I need more of you, but I can't express it. Will you listen to my pain?"

It wasn't until several visits later that Dolores finally found the courage to express all the secret resentments she harbored about her husband's overinvolvement with his family and his underinvolvement with her. Her husband was shocked but open to hearing her complaints. It was several months of further discussion before balance was restored to their marriage. Just as the psychologist had suggested, her anxiety gradually diminished until, nearly a year later, her smile returned and her anxiety was completely resolved.

Dolores's secret was something others might not be ashamed of, but secrets are something few of us are unfamiliar with. All of us have experienced secretiveness in our families in different forms: parents keep information from children and from each other, children withhold from siblings and parents, or the entire family closes ranks against the outside world. Some secret keeping is benign and reasonable, such as a surprise birthday party for a family member, or an older sibling not telling a younger sibling something that is not appropriate for his or her age.

Some secrets may also maintain healthy boundaries between generations. An adolescent, for example, may keep certain behaviors or feelings from his or her parents as part of the striving for independence. A father may not describe the graphic details of his war experience to his young son who has shown signs of being fearful and very sensitive. However, because secrets are so tied to feelings of shame, there is the danger that even secrets that serve a healthy function will inadvertently lead to a pattern of covering up anything that is uncomfortable—a pattern that bodes poorly for intimate love relations.

How Secrets Are Born—and Kept

Families differ when it comes to deciding what to reveal and what is worthy of secrecy. Dolores's family was closed and regarded nearly anything personal to be off-limits. Her family was obviously guarded and cautious. In some instances, a family seems to be open and expressive rather than secretive, but appearances are not always what they seem to be. As a young girl Anita Roddick, founder of the international Body Shop stores, lost her stepfather. Some years later she discovered that the man she called her stepfather was actually her biological father. She was the offspring of his and her mother's clandestine affair during her mother's first marriage. In similar fashion, actor Jack Nicholson grew up believing that the woman who raised him was his mother, only to find out that she was, in fact, his grandmother. The woman he thought was his sister was actually his mother.

In yet another instance of "what you see isn't necessarily all there is," Nancy's family seemed to be open and personal in their conversations. In fact, Nancy, now thirty-seven, thought that her family was the model for openness, until one evening when she was fifteen she answered the door and was confronted by a teary-eyed stranger who asked if she could come in. Her parents were in another room watching television and did not hear the knock on the door that was about to change their family. "I am your sister," the stranger announced. "What?" Nancy remembers muttering, almost involuntarily. "You're who?" Before the woman at the door could answer, Nancy requested that she wait outside while she spoke to her parents. She explained what happened next.

I was incredulous. It's odd, but I always had this feeling that something was being held back. I would ask my parents about their relationship when I was younger. There was a period of time that they were arguing constantly, and there was a pattern. As soon as the argument started, as if from prior agreement, they would leave the house and drive around in the car. "There are some things we have to talk over," my father would say, but he never explained any more than that. When I asked, he would get tense and abrupt. "There are things that are not for your ears," is all he would say.

I told my parents that there was a woman outside who says she is my sister. My father turned pale and looked at my mother with a frightened look. My mother started to cry. I found myself crying as well, and I didn't know why. I expected that they would tell me to go upstairs or something, but that's not what happened. "It is your sister," my father confessed. He got up and brought her into the house. We all sat down at the kitchen table, and my father explained that he had had an affair with a woman he hardly knew and she became pregnant. The woman insisted on having the child, and all these years he had paid child support. My half-sister told us that her mother, who had married, was dying of lung cancer. She had no intention of bringing trouble to our family. She simply wanted to see her biological father before she headed to Europe where she hoped to go into the exporting business with her boyfriend.

Later that same evening, my mother asked me to sit down for another talk. I was emotionally exhausted, but I anticipated that she was going to apologize for keeping my father's secret. It was nothing like that. Nothing at all. After what had happened earlier in the evening, I thought I knew everything about my family. Here was my mother who had kept my father's secret from me all these years. She had looked so distressed when his other daughter showed up. I thought I knew everything about them now. Now she was telling me that she'd been married once before. The marriage lasted only three years, and they were divorced.

She told me only the bare facts: he was a law student, and they had only a brief courtship before they were married. He had been married before, and he had a son who was in his custody. She was the stepparent during the period of their marriage. I could see that she was very uncomfortable talking about it, and I didn't want to push. About a week later I asked my father about it, and he just shrugged. "I don't know anything more about it than you do," he said. I had hoped that one day my parents would be more open with me about their past, but neither of them have returned to that. It is as if that night never happened, and I feel that it has put a wall between us.

Our parents are usually the first ones in our lives to set the tone in the household as to what is openly discussed, what is only for the family, and what is not discussed at all. We learn the implicit (and sometimes explicit) rules of secret keeping both from what is told to us and by observing the behavior of our parents. Even in the most innocent of homes, we are exposed to glances, a finger over the lips, a warning not to say anything to "Uncle Jack" or to the neighbors about Dad getting laid off from his job or Mom's drinking problem. We take these early lessons into adulthood; our parents' attitude about secret keeping greatly influences how we will view the world and how we will relate to a love partner. Nancy, for instance, became very sensitive to what wasn't being said in her marriage. She frequently probed her husband with questions like, "Is everything OK? Did anything else happen today? Are you sure you're telling me everything?"

In some cases, withholding can go to the heart of the relationship; these are instances in which one person keeps secret certain very personal information or the existence of a hidden double life, even criminal behavior. Disclosure generally shocks the uninformed partner. That's what happened to Katherine after she had been married to Jack, a prosperous businessman, for eight years. One day, returning from work, he suddenly announced, "I'm declaring bankruptcy. My business is hemorrhaging money, and there's no other way to stop it." He explained that his firm had been under financial pressure for a year and he wanted to tell her before she read about it.

Jack's revelation hit her like a bolt of lightning, and she felt betrayed that he hadn't told her sooner. She had been aware that he had been preoccupied and inattentive for the past few months, and she had believed him when he explained that he just had some difficult problems at work. His seemingly reasoned explanation led her to think he meant something ordinary and routine, certainly not a major financial disaster. What else had he held back? What other secrets did he have that would shock her? Here's what Jack had to say about his behavior:

> I really screwed up. Katherine is right to feel that I closed her out of my troubles. For me, it has been a way of life. I am not proud to admit it, but this is the way I've operated for years and years—for as long as I can remember. In my family my mother led us kids to believe that our father couldn't take any bad news. Growing up we learned to keep our problems from him. Either we wouldn't tell Dad at all, or we'd water things down so he wouldn't be upset. When I wanted to go to my mother with something, my sister would nix it. She told me that my mother had enough to worry about because my father didn't know half of what was going on. So, I didn't talk to my mother or father, and my sister was older than I was; she was into guys and was never around. I got used to holding secrets and continued that in my relationship with Katherine.

Not surprisingly, Jack as an adult tended not to "worry" his wife with anything that might cause her concern. In therapy, instigated at Katherine's insistence, Jack came to realize that his secrecy not only kept Katherine from really knowing him but also deprived him of Katherine's support. What's more, because he kept anything really important about him secret, there was never much to talk to her about. As Katherine said, "He was slowly turning into a stranger."

After two months in therapy, Jack announced to Katherine that he was going to the doctor, that he was feeling some discomfort in his stomach, and because his uncle and his father had had stomach cancer he wanted to check it out. Fortunately, Jack got a clean bill of health. The experience was a real turning point for him. In the past he would not have told her about his concern. "I was really worried, and Katherine was wonderfully supportive," he said. "I feel like I am part of a loving family, and it is a really good feeling. I feel pounds lighter, so much more relaxed. And we have so much more to talk about now!"

The Big Secret

As distraught as Katherine was with Jack's deceptiveness about his finances, when one partner discovers that the other is having an affair, the reaction is often unequaled by the revelation of other secrets: profound shock followed by hurt, anger, and a complete shattering of emotional security. Consider the following experience of a very attractive, twice-married, intense woman who is approaching forty:

Being a product of my times, I used sex with another man as a weapon. My husband works long hours when he really doesn't have to, and I resent it. When he comes home, he is preoccupied. He wants to watch television, read, sleep, or go on his boat. That boat is driving me crazy. I don't want to compete with a goddamn boat! I feel he would choose that boat over me without a moment of hesitation. I don't feel married. It seems he regards me as a convenience. When he is attentive, it is often in a belittling and critical manner; he makes me feel stupid and ridiculous.

One time I was relining the shelves in one of the closets very meticulously because I like things to be perfect and beautiful, and he nagged me something awful and called me a fool for wasting my time on something no one would ever see. So, either he pesters me or he ignores me, and I don't have the courage to tell him I don't like him doing that, at least not with the rage I feel. I simply have lovers. And then, when my husband continues to ignore me, to take me for granted, or comes on with his criticisms, I sit back, smile inside, and say to myself, "You're not so hot, you fool." That's my revenge!

That was working well for me, as bad as it sounds. Then my husband found out. A friend of his told him, and although he didn't believe it at first, he became suspicious. He hired a detective that followed me and took pictures of my lover and me. The pictures were graphic. Very graphic. When my husband saw the pictures, he threw up on the spot. He came home and exploded; he was enraged. He pulled one of the wooden poles right off the bed and began smashing things. The room looked as if a bomb exploded in it. I ran to call the police, and he ripped the phone off the wall. He went nuts. The next day he locked himself in the garage and ran the car; he attempted suicide. It was then that I really felt badly. That's when I realized how much I had hurt him and how much pain he was in.

The woman describing this experience was found out by telling a friend of hers, who told her husband, who then told the affair-involved woman's husband. An affair is a big secret that once revealed has very strong consequences. That's part of the problem; affairs don't lend themselves to sharing and openness. In ever-widening circles, an affair causes the person involved to operate in a guarded way in his or her primary relationship—and with others as well.

Keeping sexual activities a total secret from one's partner takes some work. Besides being caught in the act, the most dramatic disclosure of all, the ways of being found out are innumerable: cell phone bills with a printout of numbers called, an irate lover who contacts a spouse for revenge, a chance encounter with a friend, an unpredicted change in plans by a mate, and sexually transmitted diseases, which can be tough to explain if one's mate is afflicted.

This is to say nothing of changes in attitude and behavior at home that arouse a mate's suspicions. Some of those involved in affairs distance themselves from their mates, playing out a loyalty to their lovers.

Others become more amorous in an effort to compensate for their dalliance. Still others behave uncharacteristically in a variety of ways and inadvertently call attention to themselves. Diane, a woman in her early forties, has been married eighteen years and describes a period of her life when she had two affairs:

> *Although these experiences were meaningful to me, they were far from dramatic. I did not experience a grand awakening, and I wasn't particularly enamored of my sexual partners. Yet I was excited, and there was a change in me that I thought I was concealing successfully. I wasn't. One Sunday morning my husband turned to me in bed and said, "I know people change as they grow, but when you live with a woman for such a long time, you get to know her very well; you relate to me in a certain way. In the past few months, a change has come over you. I don't know what to make of it. I don't know what's wrong, but you don't seem to be with me in the same way. Did I do something to provoke this?"*

This kind of repercussion does not always occur. Some affairs may go undiscovered for a lifetime. Nonetheless, the adulterous party takes a greater risk if the marriage is close. If the outside relationship is very involved, there will more likely be subtle changes in behavior and attitude, and these are more likely to be detected in a closer marriage. Typically, at this juncture the adulterous mate will begin to lie: "Oh, it's my business troubles," or "I'm just edgy; I need a rest." If his or her mate does not buy these ambiguous answers and suspicion continues to be aroused, the lying increases as the secret expands—and the marriage deteriorates.

And, yes, sometimes a lover seeking to make trouble at home and force a separation unconsciously leaves the evidence. The affair-involved person may also sabotage him- or herself. A diary kept, letters not destroyed, an indiscreet choice of meeting places—do these have a deliberate element?

Sexual betrayal itself is bad enough—a nuclear assault on the noninvolved partner—but sometimes this most serious breach may be a message with an unconscious intent. It can be a secret that seeks to be revealed. In some relationships it may be a way of forcing the hand of a mate who refuses to acknowledge that the relationship is in trouble. Detection may also serve the purpose of those who want their mate to dissolve the relationship.

Thus, in an empty relationship, a mate may flaunt infidelity to provoke a breakup—it becomes an "open secret." When the relationship is merely troubled, an affair that is left open to discovery may be a signal to the indifferent partner to pay more attention to the relationship. Of course, most people do not willingly acknowledge that the brazenness of their sexual involvement conveys such purposes.

Nor is the intended effect usually achieved. A man who is indiscreetly conducting an affair may wish to punish his partner for past grievances, but the partner may respond with more hostility than he bargained for, perhaps with an affair of her own. A woman who is trying to push her partner into being more attentive may find herself alone when he walks out on her. In some cases, as we have seen, the hurt partner may be completely devastated and react very strongly, perhaps violently, or attempt to harm him- or herself.

Occasionally, an individual will deny a mate's obvious affair involvement because acknowledgment may be so threatening to his or her sense of emotional security that it cannot be tolerated. Thus, the noninvolved and the involved partner enter into a conspiracy of silence about the big secret.

Don Blank, a scientist in his early forties who specializes in HIV research, is very involved in his work; his idea of relaxing on the weekend is to read scientific journals and take notes. He barely takes notice that his wife is out many evenings and often comes home in disarray with alcohol on her breath, that he gets hang-ups when he picks up the phone, and that she is rarely interested in being sexual with him, yet she seems interested in watching sex scenes in movies and reading sexy stories. He seems to have unconsciously entered into a trade-off: his lover is his work; hers is an actual person, and he doesn't want to know any more than that. Probably a fair number of men and women employ the same defense of denial. Rather than confront the truth, they unconsciously join in the secret.

Some people not only collude in their partner's denial, they feel compelled to confess their sexual adventures. This is different from carrying on in a blatant manner; it is even more deliberate, and there is more choice in a voluntary confession. The motives behind voluntary confessions vary; guilt and the need to be forgiven along with a hope for a new start are the most common.

However, not all confessions are motivated by the wish for greater intimacy. I have met both men and women who have described their sexual fantasies and extramarital dalliances to create distance and alienate their partner. For some people, the fear of being engulfed is even stronger than their fear of abandonment. In other instances, a partner may confess an illicit sexual relationship to save the marriage. The confession serves to defuse the attraction of the other person and to create more vigilant conditions so that a future fall from grace is less likely. It doesn't always work out that way:

I was so hurt and angered by my husband's affair that I did nothing for four days but cry. My face was puffy and raw. I couldn't hold food; my weight fell well below normal. After those initial days—I refer to them now as the days of mourning—I started to plot and scheme. I tried to think of the best way of getting back. Howard has a brother; he is two years younger. He and his brother have been competitive all their lives. I know his brother finds me attractive. He's even made passes at me. I decided to seduce him. It worked without a hitch; his brother was most cooperative. Of course, when Howard found out—I told him—he felt as if someone had driven a truck through his stomach. I thought that would teach him. However, about six months later he got involved with one of my friends. That was it; we divorced.

The cost of confessing a sexual betrayal is obvious and immediate, but it is also long-term. Once told, a couple will have to live with the repercussions for a long time to come. In telling, we deal not only with our partner's rage and pain but also with a lengthy process of rebuilding intimacy—if it is to be rebuilt at all. So, to tell or not to tell, that is an important question. When suspicion arising out of unfaithfulness is a barrier to intimacy and the deceived partner continues to probe the issue, a frank discussion, preferably with the assistance of a therapist, is warranted. Of course, even at this juncture some people may choose not to be candid. A person remaining with a partner for expediency's sake—for instance, a wife with several children who has no hope of employment and who wants nothing from the marriage except financial support—may continue to lie in an effort to maintain the relationship. But those who wish to improve things would best consider honesty. When suspicion has become part of the marital relationship, stonewalling and further deception will serve only to create more distance and disillusion.

Some people do not reveal their secret because they want to continue the affair. They want to have both their lover and their spouse, and they know that a confession will force a choice. Others have trouble dealing with emotional turmoil and want to avoid the substantial repair process that is required following disclosure. Still others may lack the strength and sense of commitment to face their partner's accusations and the loss of face they will experience.

Confessions, like all things, may be for better or worse. Ordinarily, the chances are better for confessions that have more noble motives and worse for those that are self-serving. The self-serving reasons include using the truth about an affair as an exit visa from an unhappy marriage, revealing the affair as a weapon of revenge, or using the affair to shake up a lethargic marriage. All of these reasons for confessing have too much of a self-centered basis. In addition, there are better, less hurtful ways of approaching a marriage in trouble. If the unhappiness, for example, is overwhelming and beyond repair, just leave! If there is a lot of anger in the relationship, why not address that and the underlying hurt (it's always there!) rather than focus on hurting your mate?

In telling, the best motive is the wish to reestablish the primacy of your marriage and to remove the barrier of the kept secret. And make no mistake about it, the effects of silence about a secret life take a toll on intimacy. The telling begins an emotional journey that is arduous and not for the faint of heart. However, it also opens the door for greater integrity, depth, and closeness in a relationship.

To tell or not to tell? Couple therapists disagree. Some suggest that telling is a nonnegotiable first step toward restoring closeness. They maintain that secrecy is a form of crazy-making. Telling the truth serves the critical function of precipitating a needed marital crisis and creates the opportunity for honest dialogue. Other therapists contend that the risks are too great and advise against it unless the suspicion is high enough to warrant the risks.

My view is not hard and fast. In some situations, for some couples, the secret is best revealed. It can be the start of a new and better relationship. In other instances, the consequences can be so destructive that repair is next to impossible. In some ways it is like being told about a cancer diagnosis. Some people recover better when they are told every detail of their condition and their treatment; others are overcome by what they know and exceedingly frightened and distraught. Again, those that confess with the motive of moving the relationship to a higher plane are more likely to achieve that goal. Whether silence is chosen or a confession is made, that is, no matter how the secret is handled, there are consequences.

To maximize openness, it is wise to follow a simple rule in a love relationship: don't do anything you can't share, and be prepared to discuss everything you do. Secrets, especially ones that may involve daily deception, are sure to create distance. It is not possible to foster closeness with someone you are hiding from, confusing, and throwing offtrack.

Some Suggestions for Dealing with the Secrets in Your Life

As we have seen, most of us have grown up surrounded by secrets; they have become a natural part of our lives. The subject is far too complex for glib rules. However, some guidelines are worth considering. Children, being the least powerful members of the family, are most affected by secrets. What, how, and when to impart sensitive information to children is something both parents should discuss thoroughly and agree on before undertaking. As for adults in a love relationship, if being open and emotionally available is a goal, secrecy is a bad idea.

- Secrets between one parent and a child—whether they are subtly conveyed with a wink or obvious and blatant—are practically always problematic. Those secrets that are agreed upon implicitly may take the form of simply not informing a spouse about something pertinent that occurred with a child. The child is aware that you are keeping information from the other parent, but neither of you has explicitly agreed on the secret. In contrast, the obvious and blatant form of keeping a secret occurs when either a child or parent initiates the secret: "Don't tell Dad I got suspended from school; he'll just go ballistic and it will end up in a whole family mess." Or, "I won't tell your Dad you were arrested for shoplifting, it would only break his heart, and then he'll break your neck." Doing this sort of thing puts a child in a loyalty bind. He or she is forming an alliance with one parent to the exclusion of the other. This type of behavior carries over to adult relationships and becomes an obstacle to openness.

- When you are tempted to keep sensitive information from children or other family members, consider how the secret keeping makes you feel. Are you repeating a pattern from your own family, handed down to you by your parents? Ask yourself if something about the information feels shameful or forbidden to you. In other words, are you protecting someone else, or is this another instance of hiding from an uncomfortable truth? It is also essential to bear in mind that secrets come with a price, even if it is not exacted until years later. The effects of secrets contained in a family of origin are likely to surface in the love relationships you form in years to come.

- Secret telling is a double-edged sword. On the one hand, the process of secrecy takes its toll. It is divisive, involving insiders—those who are in on the secret—and outsiders—those who are excluded from the secret. Keeping secrets over time can require energy and active attention as well. Some secrets may be guarded by silence, and some, such as a sexual affair, require constant vigilance and further deceits. On the other hand, secrets can be connective between people, serving a loving and well-intentioned purpose. For example, if Grandma is having medical difficulties and is going in to the hospital for an MRI, it is premature to tell this to a young child until there is a clear indication of how serious the problem is. In any case, whether the underlying motive has been altruistic or not, a caution needs to be observed: revealing a sensitive secret requires empathy on the part of the recipient as well as the secret holder. If there is not sufficient connection between people, a genuine relationship that will support the process of working through the impact of the secret, the revelation can be harmful and reckless.

- Don't put a spin on your secret keeping by calling it "your need for privacy." This is not to say that neither you nor your partner is entitled to privacy. However, privacy is different from secrecy. Our right to privacy involves our protection from intrusion—we close the door to the bathroom, we expect that our phone calls are not taped and that our personal property is not searched, we want some time to ourselves without interruption—those are some examples of privacy. Secrecy is a deliberate concealment of information that makes a difference in a loved one's life. It is consequential.

- Consider the thoughts and experiences about which you are most ashamed. Pretend someone else has confessed these things to you. What counsel would you offer that person? Are you more benevolent to this "other person" than toward yourself? Demonstrate confidence in your partner by discussing one or more of these experiences with him or her.

- The negative aspects of secrecy on children may stay underground for years and are most likely to be triggered in adult love relations. Go back in time to your family of origin. What patterns of secrecy were apparent as you reflect back? Consider the subtle as well as the obvious attempts at secrecy. It may have been one of your parents' overuse of alcohol, secrets that you had with one or the other of your parents, or certain subjects that were not talked about. Discuss these patterns with your partner, and see if you can bring the discussion into how your family secrets have affected your current love relationship.

In sum, we should be clear with ourselves that secrecy (which practically always requires maintenance in the form of deception and silence) narrows the possibilities of connection between lovers.

7

WHEN WORDS FAIL

Whenever our verbal and nonverbal forms of communication are discrepant—when our words convey one message but our tone of voice or body another—we are likely to arouse suspicion and confusion in the listener. To foster openness words and actions must be consistent. Simply put, the old adage "It is not only what you say, but how you say it" is particularly important between lovers.

In the drama of open relating, the nonverbal dimension is particularly important. Research indicates that about 70 percent of our communication with others is carried out on a nonverbal level. Analysis of slow-motion films of couples in various situations reveals that the two individuals continually "speak" to each other in nonverbal modes (gestures, actions, facial expressions, and the like). When couples are in discord, for example, messages abound without their uttering a word. Strategic avoidance of eye contact, the utilization of eye rolling and expressions of disgust, the tendency to glare at one's partner, clenched hands, quick movements—all of these are powerful indications of negativity. Stylistic aspects of what is being said are crucial as well. Tone of voice, volume, sarcasm, and pacing of what is said—all make a difference, as we shall see.

While negativity is not something most of us are enthusiastic about confronting, if it is out there and direct, we can at least engage it and work toward resolution. However, if the accompanying words are not consistent with the nonverbal component, they are less likely to lead toward resolution. In fact, the situation is more likely to lead to "crazy-making," hearing one thing but receiving another message that conveys something else—as the following exchange demonstrates. Connie and Sam had been married for two years; they had no children. Connie had just been offered a promotion at her job, with more responsibility and a substantial increase in salary. That day when she returned home she met her husband at the door and bubbled her good news.

Sam, with a long face, said, "Gee, that's wonderful. I'm really glad for you." Connie was puzzled. "You say you're glad but your face doesn't show it. Is something wrong?" Sam folded his arms across his chest and took a step back. "No, I'm fine," he said in a flat tone. "Are you sure?" Connie asked once again. "You seem like you're not really happy." "I'm happy, damn it!" Sam insisted. "I'm happy."

The remainder of the evening was strained. In the morning Sam confessed. "I guess I was jealous," he said softly, looking at Connie with his hand on her shoulder. "I have been busting my back trying to get ahead in my job, and I haven't received so much as a thank-you from my boss. I feel unappreciated. Now you tell me you have been offered a major promotion. It took me back initially. But I thought about it some more last night, and I am happy for you. I really am. It just took me a little time to get myself together. Congratulations!"

Connie smiled at Sam. "Thank you," she said. "Your support means a lot to me."

By revisiting the exchange of the previous evening with a different attitude that was conveyed not only by the honesty of his words but by the very different physical gestures and tone—which supported his words—Sam created a very different outcome.

Behavioral scientists have found that most of us rely on nonverbal behavior in all of our exchanges, but it is particularly telling as a means of communicating attraction or disdain in a social encounter. The face, followed by the hands and feet, are considered sources of the most fertile cues to the meaning of a communication. For example, if a husband suggests sex to his wife and she says no, the meaning of her response can be clarified by the facial expression that accompanies it. If, as she says no, she smiles, she may be signaling: "Don't just ask, seduce me, be playful." If she frowns and presses her lips together angrily, her refusal is scornful and decisive: "I'm angry. How can you expect me to be intimate after embarrassing me last night!" If she offers a meek no, exhaling emphatically, as she responds, her decline may be more delay than refusal: "I'm pretty tired now, but perhaps later—or tomorrow." In each instance, the same verbal response was given, but the unspoken accompaniment relayed a very different message.

In the same vein, if a woman asks a man his feelings about her, his response of "I love you" would be greatly strengthened if he maintained eye contact while speaking. Moving his open hands toward her would say something very different than clenching his fists when he answers. And sitting with his knees tightly closed together would express a very different feeling than would his answering her question while reaching toward her with open, outstretched legs.

Related to the nonverbal aspect of a communication is the style of delivery. Julius and Barbara Fast, in *Talking Between the Lines*, focus their sharp gaze on the tone, rhythm, and volume of voice, as well the emotional overlay we give to words—sarcasm, tenderness, irritability.

Consider the simple factual statement, "I cleared the kitchen table." A partner may say this in a haughty tone of voice that conveys, "I'm so much better than you; you're such a slob," or a friendly tone that says, "I'm glad to be able to help out." An intimate may request help cleaning the table in a heavy voice that says, "I'm exhausted, please lend a hand"; a hurt tone that says, "Poor me, you always leave me the dirty work"; or an angry tone that says, "Damn you, I resent having to remind you about cleaning up."

The rhythm of a message—where the emphasis is placed and the pacing—adds another dimension. Even Muriel, a three-year-old child, is sensitive to these undercurrents. Muriel's parents consider themselves civilized; they never fight in front of Muriel. "In fact," they boast, "we rarely even raise our voices in front of her." Yet Muriel senses that Mom and Dad are frequently angry.

"Don't be mad!" she pleads defensively when she tears her new dress. "Dad's not mad, honey. Mom should have saved the dress for a special occasion." Turning to his wife, he says, "I'm sure you can sew that tear dear."

It seems a simple, even a loving request. The word "dear" is even thrown in. But Muriel hears nothing simple or loving in the statement. She hears the tight anger in her father's voice, his emphasis on "you," the slight but strategic pause before "dear."

On the surface, Muriel's parents are communicating that everything is fine; this is a loving, cooperative family. But the manner of speaking, the music of the words, indicate that everything is not fine. Muriel is sensitized to these continual contradictions, and she reacts by developing an apologetic posture in an attempt to relieve her own anxiety and assuage the controlled rage between her parents. Rather than deal with their feelings openly, her parents have become expert in engaging in pseudo openness.

Just as tone, rhythm, and accompanying emotion affect the meaning of a communication, volume also discloses a tremendous amount about an interaction. For example, a person of high status may raise his or her voice to someone of lower status; an officer may yell at an enlisted man, an executive at an underling, a teacher at a student, a parent at a child, a husband at a wife, a wife at a husband, depending on who is feeling superior at a particular time.

In contrast, volume often drops off, perhaps even to a whisper, under certain circumstances. A lowered voice may convey caring, as when we comfort the bereaved; intimacy, by signaling, "What I have to say is for your ears alone"; the quiet before the storm, when the lowered volume is accompanied by slow, painstakingly deliberate speech through clenched teeth; or fear, as in, "Don't attack me. I am lowering my voice to demonstrate my defenselessness."

Of course, as with other stylistic and nonverbal aspects of relating, meaning may vary depending on culture and background. In one family, soft, melodic speech with only minor animation is associated with calm, loving messages. In another family, the voice and energy level are higher. Family members yell continually, orchestrating their speech with flailing arms. In this family, these are the signals of love and warmth.

In many cases, we simply become so accustomed to our partner's non-verbal and stylistic signs that they cease to affect us on a conscious level. Sometimes, too, we deliberately screen them out or disregard them, either from impatience or misunderstood intent. Consider the following exchange:

The scene takes place around midnight at a house party. Gail is tired and eager to return home; her six-year-old has been ill, and she was up several times the previous night comforting him. Gail's husband, David, is seated next to Gloria, a young, attractive woman, and is heavily engrossed in conversation. Gail positions herself so that she is able to make eye contact with David, and then she taps her foot impatiently while motioning toward the door with her head.

DAVID: (to himself) *She's jealous; she wants me to leave.*

GLORIA: (to herself) *His wife wants him to leave. Let's see what kind of choice he makes.*

With this unspoken challenge, Gloria leans toward David and tosses her head back, letting her hair fall freely in a provocative manner.

DAVID: (turns his back to his wife and thinks to himself) *She's not going to order me around.*

GAIL: (to herself) *What a selfish bastard! He knows I'm tired. Wait until we get home.*

Gail and David's spat illustrates the importance of being sensitive to your partner's silent signals. In a very brief, wordless exchange, a plea to leave was sent and misunderstood, feelings of jealousy were inter-preted, Gloria offered a challenge, and David reacted as if his "man-hood" was at stake. Feelings of anger, seduction, hurt, and confusion ensued.

On other occasions, it is not so much that couples misread the non-verbal cues as that the nonverbal aspect of the message contradicts the spoken word. Larry may say to his wife, "I see," while glancing at the morning newspaper. Allen may tell his wife, "I like your hair," but say it in a flippant manner while focusing his attention elsewhere. The partners of both Allen and Larry have good cause to wonder about the reliability of the messages they are receiving. These are not the types of messages that influence them to feel safe enough to reveal themselves.

Sometimes the discrepancy between what we say and how we say it is a signal that there is an underlying problem in the relationship. Confronting the contradictions and discussing them may well bring to awareness unrecognized feelings, gripes, and desires. Perhaps Larry was in effect saying, "You don't give me your full attention when I am speaking with you, so I am not going to give you mine!" However, in this instance Larry was simply more interested in the morning's news than in viewing what his wife was showing him. He could have been honest and said that he really wanted to finish what he was reading, saying something like: "I'd like to take a closer look. I'll be finished in twenty minutes, and I'll be ready to give you my full attention." If his wife felt strongly about having his attention immediately, she could have made this known. If she didn't, she could have respected Larry's desire for a delay.

Larry and his wife were being overly polite in an attempt to create an impression that is unreasonable: we are *always* desirous of contact with each other. In actuality, both Larry and his wife were collecting "resentment stamps" in regard to this issue. Many couples are burdened with this and similar relationship-eroding demands. Most often, these demands are evident in nonverbal behavior.

Recognizing and countering the irrational premises in a relationship can be aided immensely by paying attention to *how* a message is conveyed as well as to the content of the message. This is not to suggest that intimates should immediately clobber each other with "Aha, I caught you in a lie." Instead, a candid, nonaccusatory discussion of the contradiction can be used to foster greater openness in the relationship. It is a mistake to think that you can say to yourself, "I don't believe him (her)" and not have that influence the intimacy of your love relationship.

Actions Speak Louder than Words

When actions are consistent with words, we may not like what is being conveyed, but at least the message is clear. However, when a person says something—as we have seen with Larry—and his or her actions signal something else, openness becomes a casualty. For example, a wife says to her husband that she is completely understanding of their strained financial situation and that she will exercise the same frugality that he has been applying until they get out from under their debt. The husband expresses his appreciation and feels reassured. The next month, and the month after that, he checks the itemized list on his credit card statement only to find a number of seemingly unnecessary expenses incurred by his wife that substantially add to their debt.

The husband feels irritated and resentful because his wife's behavior has not been true to her words. He brings up the issue, and she explains that the expenses were necessary but that she is being as careful as she can be. She reassures him that she is aware of the mounting debt. The next month and the month following, once again some of the expenditures seem unnecessary and the total cost is too high for the husband. Again, the husband gives his wife the benefit of the doubt regarding the nature of the expenses. But buying their four-year-old son pants that cost eighty dollars? Yet another pocketbook? He is unable to reconcile these kinds of expenses at such a difficult financial moment. This time he fears that a nasty argument would take place if he brings up his concern yet again. He feels this way because he could see that his wife was barely tolerant when he voiced his concern the last time.

Despite his apprehension, it would be wise to revisit the issue with his wife and once again attempt to come to an understanding. Somewhere in the discussion the husband might even consider the possibility that there is an underlying issue—perhaps his wife has a beef with him and that is influencing her lack of cooperation. However, in this instance, and in many others of this type, the issue is sensitive—the husband doesn't want to feel like a failure by constantly bringing up that he is not able to handle the bills, nor does he want to create discord— so he avoids opening a discussion. In addition, the husband now feels that his wife is merely paying him lip service. Even if she agrees to be more budget-minded, he has no confidence that her actions will support her words.

Not bringing up the issue for serious discussion is a mistake. Avoiding issues that are troublesome is anything but benign. If these issues are not worked out, even if they are difficult, resentment will build up and create a major obstacle to openness. After some time of this behavior, the underlying anger gets between the couple in small increments that eventually become insurmountable. It is as if he or she is adding a brick to the wall between them until the wall is impenetrable.

In another variation, the resentment is built up and may lead one partner to consciously or unconsciously "get back at" the other, either by doing something that the other partner doesn't like or by not doing something that is desired by the other partner. Usually, this leads to less cooperation and more ill will. In contrast, if the partner whose actions belie his or her words simply disagreed with the request and explained the basis for that or offered an alternative solution—"I will get a job," or "I will not use a house-cleaning service, but I want to keep my gym membership"—there is basis for an open discussion. Even if the partner admitted that she had gone overboard—"I just couldn't resist that bag, it was a great buy, and I have a weakness for that style"—it would be better than insisting that she is offering full cooperation when she is not.

While most inconsistencies between word and deed (or the manner in which a message is conveyed) may seem minor, they can have a powerful impact. If one partner tells the other, "You are the most important person in my life and my top priority," but in daily behavior is selfish, inconsiderate, and irritable, the message that is conveyed is something like this: "Your feelings and wishes are not important to me, and you can't count on what I say." The partner who is conveying the loving message but is not *being* loving actually is setting up a type of "Chinese water torture." The acts or "drops" that constitute the torture may seem inconsequential, but they are anything but innocent. Over time, not feeling loved, a couple will find they have nothing left to say to each other—and they may not even realize why. Here is the accounting of one woman:

It's been four years since Bob and I have not been close, and I still cannot be very exact about when an awareness of trouble began in the marriage. It was very subtle, like there had been a barely perceptible eroding of the foundation, weakening my commitment in innocent increments. I began feeling like I wanted to be away from Bob more than I felt like being with him. At first I figured it was just overwork and I cut back. But that didn't really help. I couldn't pin my dissatisfaction on something. I complained about a bunch of things, but in my heart I knew that wasn't it. I knew that if I were in love with somebody, the things I complained about wouldn't be a problem. I knew that, but I was frightened to admit it to myself. The implications weren't good. For about two years I just stumbled along, there were no major confrontations between us, but I wasn't happy. I started more seriously thinking about leaving. All this time Bob didn't really know the degree of my unhappiness; he thought I was just sounding off in an ordinary way. He's a good guy. I can't say he abused me or that he even did anything really bad. How do you tell him you've just fallen out of love?

Finally, out of desperation, I consulted with a psychologist. I didn't even tell Bob initially. I went to the psychologist for more than a month before I told him. The psychologist was gently insistent that we explore why I was so uncomfortable telling Bob I had begun treatment. He felt that the same dynamic was probably behind my not telling him that had brought on the trouble in the first place. And he was right. I didn't tell Bob because I just didn't feel that his reaction would be sincere. He would express concern initially, but by the next week it would be as if I hadn't told him. It would be out of his mind. That's how things were with him. I regarded it as a false sincerity. No follow-up. It's like when I told him a few months ago that I had a really important meeting at work and I was really stressed over it. He expressed real concern. Then the day of the meeting came, and he said nothing. The next day, he said nothing. It was as if the issue never existed. Can he really care about me and not ask? I mean that little example and variations on it happened numerous times. I thought I had become used to it. But after a few months of therapy I realized that it was that sort of thing that had dampened my feelings for Bob. I had been looking for some big dramatic event. It was the small things that just chipped away at my feelings.

Not only are these everyday issues difficult to identify, after a while they are often a confusing source of discomfort for the disillusioned partner. As with the woman in the previous example, the discomfort surfaces gradually and indirectly through irritation, withdrawal, or sometimes through a dramatic betrayal such as an affair. In the beginning, though, uncoupling occurs in a subtle, private manner. It is an unexpressed feeling growing in the psyche of a disgruntled lover like a deadly cancer.

The disillusioned partner may be discomforted, but he or she may fall into the same pattern as the resented partner; affection may be expressed that gives a false impression; clandestine support may be sought with a trusted ally. The breach is usually deepened as discontent begins to surface indirectly, through the words and deeds of everyday life: "I wish you would start being on time"; "I can't stand it when you speak with food in your mouth"; "How can you sit around all day and not be productive?" The emphasis is on the other person's daily failings; the complaints are real but miss the degree of discontent. Usually, the responses to the complaints are at the level at which they were issued: minor grumbles are matched with grumblelike retorts. And so the deception, a deception of true feelings, continues to confuse and muddle the underlying schism between the two people.

Sarcasm, Denial, and Other Ways of Avoiding Openness

Many people use sarcasm without being aware of how damaging it is to openness in their relationship. Examples of sarcasm range from good-natured kidding to the sadistic. The good-natured version is often said at the speaker's expense and is self-deprecating. Mark has a terrible sense of direction and makes comments like this: "You know how terrific I am with directions, I should get a job as a tour guide in New York. . . ." Remarks like these do not inhibit openness; in fact, they may foster it by giving a couple "permission" to not take their foibles so seriously.

Of course, sarcasm can be directed at a partner as well. There are people who love good-natured kidding, whether it is at their expense or intended for their partner. Elliot and Marlene, for example, often trade urbane double entendres that allow them to be suggestive without being lewd. Their banter of veiled meanings has become a marvelous game of matched wits that delights their friends as well as each other. Elliot is an engineer and an inventor. Marlene is a former model who loves to sun herself. Here is a sampling from a day they were out with friends and mildly irritated with each other: "The only reason I got married," Marlene quips with a broad smile, "is suntan lotion. There are parts of my back I just can't reach and I need help." "If I had known that," Elliot counters, "I would have invented a portable back gadget just for that purpose; it would have saved us both a lot of trouble." On other occasions they may tease each other about sex, come on to each other, flirt, or drop hints that are personal to them.

This type of teasing and being playful works for them. There are others who resent it vehemently. How do you know how far to go with these types of remarks? The answer is simple: sarcasm and good-natured kidding are not constructive if your partner reacts unfavorably. Judge what you say not by how you feel about it but by the effect it has on your partner.

For those who are uneasy about expressing their feelings, sarcasm can be used (and abused) as transparent camouflage. For example, Fred often leaves his dirty clothes on the floor rather than picking up after himself. Dina, his wife, is getting tired of his inconsideration. Instead of saying openly and directly, "Fred, I'd like you to pick up your own clothes and put them in the hamper," she uses sarcasm. As she stoops down to pick up his clothes, she says, "I wonder if your mother is relieved to have me doing this now." Later, Dina complains to a friend, "I tell my husband how I feel, but he never responds. He really is spoiled."

While sarcasm in its milder forms can be playful or a method of avoiding responsibility for how you really feel, it can also be used as a sadistic weapon that can be extremely destructive and cutting. One woman, very attractive and a master at precisely timed piercing remarks, used sarcasm to ridicule almost everything her husband did. She was especially contemptuous of his job as an FBI agent. One day he was looking for a pair of socks and was very frustrated. His wife characteristically seized the opportunity and said, "That's just what this country needs, a detective who can't even find his socks. You really inspire confidence." When he finally threw a tantrum and emptied the contents of his drawer, his wife continued leafing through her magazine and calmly remarked, "That's definitely a sign of your maturity. You should write a memo to your boss, describing your behavior; maybe he'll promote you to a higher grade." And when he was tested along with his wife in regard to their difficulty conceiving, his sperm count came back low. "Oh, that's just great," she said. "I am married to an FBI agent who shoots blanks!" A month after the last comment, he filed for divorce.

The most sensitive area for many couples is sex. Sarcasm and non-verbal behavior is particularly powerful in this area. Here is an experience that occurred several years ago and is recounted by Todd, who notes that it remains as vivid (and hurtful) as if it had happened yesterday:

Yvette was lying on the bed in this very sexy nightgown, but she had this tense facial expression that was confusing to me; it wasn't clear if she wanted to make love or she was setting up some kind of test for me. The previous day we had had this big argument, and she felt really put down by me. Honestly, she had a point. I was so frustrated with her that I said some nasty things that I regret. Was this a makeup offer, or was it some kind of retaliation?

I got into bed and I had an erection, and then I lost it. I guess I did not find her demeanor to be that sexy. "I'm pretty tired," I said. "Come on, Todd," she said. "Don't let me down." She emphasized the word down *as she glanced at my flaccid penis. I kissed her but with a growing apprehension rather than passion. "That's not much of a kiss," she said. "You seemed like a big guy yesterday," she hissed in a tone dripping with sarcasm. "Today, somehow you don't seem so big." This time she glared at my groin. Then she went to stimulate me, but her kissing and touching were rapid and conveyed impatience and tenseness more than affection and pleasure. I remained flaccid. "Why don't you do something?" Yvette snapped. "I'm trying," I replied meekly. "Then try harder," she commanded. "You certainly didn't have any problem screwing me yesterday; I don't see why you can't get it up today. . . ."*

Not only did Yvette's comments negatively influence Todd on that particular occasion, but several years later he still remains somewhat apprehensive about their lovemaking. Moreover, when Yvette asks him if something is the matter, he denies that there is, making up some sort of excuse. Yvette used sarcasm in a very sensitive area to retaliate for the hurt she felt in her previous argument with Todd, rather than deal with her hurt feelings directly. Todd, in turn, has withdrawn from Yvette rather than deal with the hurt and embarrassment he is experiencing.

Here are a variety of miscellaneous ways that interfere with authenticity and openness:

"Yes, but":

Ted and Florence have been discussing a vacation in Florida. Both agree that money is tight.

TED: *I think flying instead of driving is too rich for our budget right now. Let's drive down. We can take our time and make it fun.*

FLORENCE: *You're right, but we can work it out.*

Are they flying or driving? When one partner brings in the "but," the other partner is very likely to be confused and, worse yet, to feel discounted.

Then there's the put-off:

Alex was telling Marie about something that she said the previous evening that hurt his feelings. Halfway through his statement, she interjected in a sharp, curt tone. "All right," she said. "I get it." Her words said one thing, but her tone indicated something else: "I don't care enough to hear about this." Understandably, Alex felt cut off.

Another, more subtle message:

JILL: (to her husband) *I wish you'd show me how to con guys into paying as much attention to me at work as you get from the women at your job.*

Is Jill asking her husband for advice or putting him down for the way he flirts at work? When her husband raises that very question, Jill responds defensively: "Hey, can't you take a little teasing. I was only kidding. I wouldn't have said it if I really was bothered." On the other hand, if her husband accepted the remark as teasing, she could say later, "I try to tell you something in a way that isn't confrontational and you never take me seriously." In other words, there is a catch-22 to these tricky remarks: no matter how the listener responds, the speaker can always back off by saying, "Oh, I didn't mean it that way."

Mixed messages generally represent a pattern of avoiding responsibility for what you are really thinking and feeling. Indeed, a pattern of mixed messages to disguise true feelings and intentions inevitably leads to guardedness in relationships. However, there are times when mixed messages add sparkle and fun to conversations. When Groucho Marx tapped his cigar, wiggled his mustache, and leered at a sexy woman, "Come up and see my etchings some time," he wasn't interested in introducing her to his art collection. Those kind of flirtatious, playful messages between couples are fun. They allow a couple to be suggestive and sexy without being lewd. Indeed, the banter of veiled meanings and matched wit can be connective and great fun.

Putting the *What* and *How* of Openness Together

The following are awareness-building experiences designed to alert couples to their stylistic and nonverbal signals. The intent is to develop consistency between *what* is said and *how* it is said.

- Both partners are to sit together with eyes closed throughout. (Eliminating vision forces a heightened auditory sensitivity.) Initiate a discussion of importance to the relationship. You may discuss division of marital/parental responsibilities, in-laws, feelings about a recent issue, or any other topic of mutual interest. As you do this, focus your attention on your own and your partner's voice. See if you can listen as if the other person were speaking in an unfamiliar language. Try to understand the message by listening to the emphasis, tone, rhythm, etc. Do this for about fifteen minutes. Now discuss what you noticed about your own voice and your partner's. Be very specific in your commentary. What is the voice like? Is it strong or weak, clear or unclear, harsh or mellow? Is it judging, complaining, angry, pleading, hurt? Does the style fit the content? What effect does the voice and its stylistic variation have on you?

- In this experience, the goal is to highlight inconsistencies in what the message receiver *hears* and what he or she *sees* expressed through body language. Each partner will alternate expressing a sentiment and canceling its meaning with a gesture, grimace, motion, facial expression, or some other non-verbal behavior. The sentiments, expressed in your own words, should include: (1) an expression of approval (for example, as Jill compliments Mark on a decision he has made, she looks down, shakes her head side to side, and plants her hands on her hips—all actions that signal disapproval and resignation to Mark); (2) a caring expression; and (3) an expression of availability (to problem solve, help with chores, do a favor, honor a request). Be aware of how you feel as you send and receive these inconsistent messages. Discuss exactly what you and your partner do to cancel the verbal messages. Do any of these ways of canceling feel familiar? After completing the discussion, change the body language and express approval, caring, and availability again. This time match the spoken word with the unspoken signals. Discuss the difference. On a daily basis, be alert to the unspoken cues of your spouse that express approval, caring, and availability.

- Take turns repeating the following three negative expressions, observing yourself (in a full-length mirror) and each other as you do so: "Right now I don't like you"; "You're being unreasonable, and I won't continue listening"; "I suspect that you're lying." Make each statement loudly, forcefully. At the same time, be aware of how you are standing, what your body posture is like, how you hold your head, and so on. An intimate may offer a suggestion to be incorporated into the expression. Doreen, observing Mitch, might say, "Look past me when you say, 'I don't like you.' That's what usually happens when you're mad." Demonstrate, if necessary. After each partner has had an opportunity to act out the negative emotions associated with dissatisfaction, discuss other unspoken negative expressions that each has noticed in the other. You might focus on such issues as impatience, skepticism, annoyance, hurt, boredom, and inattentiveness.

Note: as a general rule, both verbal and nonverbal means are effective for expressing positive feelings. Negative expressions, which are more apt to be emotion-laden, are best expressed mainly through words. This is important because there is a tendency in delivering a negative expression to avoid responsibility for it. For example, Frank is angry with Barbara. He glares at her and speaks in a halting, intense manner. When Barbara asks him if something is bothering him, Frank self-righteously maintains that everything is fine.

The sender of most negative, subtle messages has the ability to avoid a resolution if confronted by hiding behind the camouflage of misunderstanding and denial. Therefore, in the interest of clear relating, couples are wise to articulate negative messages so that the sender has responsibility for the message and the receiver can respond unambiguously to the complaint.

Whether the message being conveyed is negative or positive, if the nonverbal or stylistic elements are not consistent with the spoken word, it is a strong indication that the speaker is uncomfortable with what he or she is conveying. The underlying message may be: "If I told you how I really feel, you wouldn't approve. I might lose your love, respect, admiration." In the interest of openness, I strongly suggest that you discuss these underlying issues.

8

FIGHTING FOR INTIMACY

Rather than honestly put their most sensitive and conflict-laden issues forward for discussion, couples often mask (or suppress) them in an effort to protect their vulnerability and avoid intimacy. The fights that ensue are pointless and counterproductive. Camouflaged emotional volleys are akin to smoking and high cholesterol as risk factors for heart disease—the more intense and prolonged, the greater the danger. Eventually, the relationship will lapse into "illness" or divorce.

The German philosopher Arthur Schopenhauer told the story of two porcupines huddled together on a cold winter's night. As the temperature dropped, the animals moved closer together. But then there was a problem: each kept getting pricked by the other's quills. Finally, with much shifting and shuffling and changing positions, they managed to work out an equilibrium whereby each got maximum warmth with a minimum of painful pricking from the other. Many couples have something in common with the huddling porcupines. They want to achieve and maintain a kind of equilibrium: warmth and closeness but without the sometimes agonizing "pricking" that comes from continuous interaction with another human being.

Some individuals are so desirous of "smoothing the rub" and creating perfect harmony that they keep many grudges hidden from their partner. Unlike those individuals who are excessively and indiscriminately negative, these individuals are unwilling or unable to express their displeasure toward their partner. They are reluctant either to place definite limits on what they will and will not tolerate or to resolve the issues between them. Commonly, their grievance may be rationalized: "Oh, it really doesn't matter anyway"; even the fact that problems exist may be denied.

In most instances of this sort, individuals choose to withdraw rather than confront the problem and risk a disturbance of the peace. Often, this occurs because the withdrawing partner has not developed appropriately assertive behaviors or does not want to work through the issues and foster greater closeness; therefore, he or she avoids telling the other partner calmly (or not so calmly) of his or her displeasure with the way things are going between them.

The other partner, on the other hand, often compounds the problem further by collaborating in the cover-up. It is not often that the displeased partner is alone in his or her unhappiness; the other partner is often aware of the unhappiness and has his or her dissatisfaction as well. He or she has entered into a conspiracy of silence in the relationship. Indeed, the more vocal partner, the one with the more dominant personality in the relationship, is usually invested in his or her partner not being vocal about what is really going on.

A classic example of underlying and indirectly expressed hostility involves Mr. and Mrs. Herbert Blake, a prosperous suburban couple who have been married for fifteen years. They have two teenaged children and are socially popular. Mr. Blake is an executive with a substantial income; his wife is well dressed, plays excellent bridge, and does more than her share of local charity work. Everybody thinks they have a fine marriage. In addition, both are considered socially desirable, well-informed conversationalists. But at home Mr. Blake rarely says much; to keep the peace, he goes along with whatever his wife wants.

One day shortly after leaving for an all-day charity event, Mrs. Blake returns home unexpectedly for the raffle tickets left on the kitchen table and discovers Herbert in bed with another woman. At first she is incredulous, then horrified. In the marital crisis that follows, Mrs. Blake learns that the "silent treatment" she has been receiving all these years is not cooperation or strength but hostility camouflaged by phony and misleading compliance. Mr. Blake admits that he has never leveled with his wife, never clearly conveyed his feelings about the way she dominated most of the family decisions. Though it riled him when she decided what they should do to have fun or to be creative, almost invariably he went along with her ideas. On the few occasions when he did protest mildly—always without making the depth of his feelings clear—he found that his wife became even more aggressive. So he became quieter. He puts it this way:

> *I felt it undignified to get in there and really let her have it. I grew up in a family with a lot of screaming. I remember the hurts, the insults, the pain, and the meanness very vividly. I didn't want that in my life. I didn't want to get embroiled in the kind of rage my parents expressed. Yet being dominated, being bossed around, and feeling like a doormat really bothered me. I chose an affair—with a particularly passive woman, by the way—as an equalizer. Taking her to the house, of course, was stupid. Although if I'm going to be totally honest, I must admit to having mixed emotions about being caught, part of it being, "Good, you bitch, at least you can unmistakably see you are not dealing with the village idiot!" I feel curiously relieved.*

The Herbert Blakes among us, both male and female, share a common deceptive belief: it isn't "gentlemanly," it isn't "feminine," to emotionally express dissatisfaction and annoyance; it isn't nice; it isn't mature. This is supposed to be the age of reason, so we must always feel civilized and reasonable! In an ideal situation, resolving differences is best if conducted in a harmonious manner, but this need not always be so. Perfect harmony is unrealistic and highly unlikely; simply sharing space and time together, having different interests and preferences, individuals limit each other's choices. Like the petri dishes of a high school biology class, relationships provide fertile ground in which the germs of conflict can flourish. This does not mean that brawling is being advocated. Rather, issues between a couple—whether deep-seated or superficial—are inevitable and must be recognized. To completely avoid or deny the undercurrent in a relationship is a sure way to deaden it.

Some fascinating experiments document this thesis. In a series of famous studies, psychologist Harry F. Harlow reared several generations of monkeys and demonstrated that those that were raised by nonfighting monkey mothers would not make love. Another well-known researcher, Konrad Lorenz, found that birds and animals that did not hold back their aggression became staunch friends. Likewise, Harvard psychoanalyst Erik Erikson and noted psychologist and author George Bach blame the failure to achieve intimacy on the inability to engage in controversy and open (even if heated) discussion.

Today, almost everyone has heard of a separation that seems to be a sudden and unexpected outcome in a tranquil relationship. Of course, this is rarely the case; a closer look at these relationships reveals not fulfillment marred by a crisis but a profound and cancerous unhappiness resembling that of the characters in Elia Kazan's novel *The Arrangement*. In this story, the protagonist has become increasingly (but quietly) dissatisfied with his marriage, and at forty-three he engages in a serious affair with a younger woman. He is confused by his behavior and feels guilty because he either doesn't understand or won't acknowledge that his wife's good nature is leaving him unfulfilled and conflicted. His wife, true to her helping nature, arranges a plan, a different "style of life" for the two of them, with the hope it will draw them together and rid her husband of his misery. The husband complies—out of passivity or sheer exhaustion—and for almost a year they live in a way designed to protect the couple (him!) from the conflicts that threaten their illusory togetherness. The arrangement, appropriately called "the fortress," backfires: instead of eliminating the husband's marital discontent, it causes him to become even more passive and, finally, unable to respond sexually.

During the eleven-month fortress period, the husband and wife are the envy of all their friends. The wife's emphasis on the "pure" life and the husband's surface receptiveness project an image of sharing, togetherness, and unusual devotion. Below the surface, however, is a serious dilemma, for the dream of "happily ever after" is not shared; it belongs only to the wife. A near-fatal auto accident, which is recognized by the husband as a suicide gesture, forcefully shatters the togetherness fantasy. The husband, after his recovery, leaves his wife.

Perhaps with less drama but through an essentially similar process, many couples grow apart. Although they appear to share common goals, their "arrangement" is based on one person's vision. The other is silently veering off in a different direction. Openness, self-revelation, and putting feelings forward in a straightforward manner can be the force that prevents the buildup of a fortress; that is to say, every issue—minor as well as major, long-term as well as brief—involves some emotional reaction. Whether the emotion evolves into alienation or increased togetherness is dependent on how it is approached. Indeed, the failure to deal constructively and compassionately with differences and the issues between and within the couple is the single most powerful force in relationship deterioration.

For some, the "solution" to unresolved conflict is a double life: an emotional divorce from one's partner (preserving the convenience of family life) along with a search for emotional union outside the relationship. The "other man" or "other woman" is sought as a diversion to make a dreary relationship tolerable. The relief is merely temporary and resolves nothing. Other couples react to their emotional divorce by establishing a pseudo relationship, wherein the satisfaction derived from outside activities masks the emptiness within. Still others engage in major battles during which nothing gets settled and both partners are emotionally (and sometimes physically!) bruised. Typically these battles take on the characteristics of war.

In a war there is only one goal: victory. And victory is achieved through destruction. In a relationship the goal of a battle is the opposite: an attempt to improve openness and closeness. Consequently, to "win" a marital conflict is an illusion: it is an empty victory because it encourages deceptions in future disagreements ("I'm not about to let him use this against me"), fosters needless pessimism ("What's the use?

I can never get my point across; this relationship will never work"), and will very likely lead to retaliation to "even the score." In some warlike battles, after many disturbing fights, partners may even give up hope of any individual gain and focus instead on limiting the other's advantage. In essence, rather than anything being settled, disagreements serve to torture the other partner.

Bringing in the Children

Sometimes, when couples have offspring, the relationship may erupt into a war in which the children may be both the ammunition and the primary casualties. Or guerilla warfare may result, with each partner lunging at the other's weak spots. Here is an illustration:

The Hansons, who are on a family vacation, have just finished dinner and are leaving the restaurant. Doreen goes to the bathroom. Alfred and their six-year-old son, Sam, wait for her by the front counter. When Doreen returns, she notices that Sam has a book of matches in his hand. "What is that?" she asks her husband with barely concealed disdain.

"Oh, Sam wanted a remembrance of the restaurant," Alfred replies.

"Matches?" Doreen admonishes angrily while taking Sam's hand and nudging him closer to her. "What kind of judgment is that? Sam is only six; he shouldn't have matches."

Sam glances at his father sheepishly and returns the matches to the dish on the counter.

Now Alfred becomes angry. He puts his arm around Sam as if Sam was his little buddy and nudges Sam toward him. "What do you think he is going to do, burn the house down?" he snaps. "He doesn't even know what to do with matches; he just wanted to have a little souvenir. You are such a downer!"

Alfred and Doreen continue the argument on the walk back to their cottage as if Sam was not with them. Shortly before they arrive, Sam begins crying and pleads with them to stop. "If you don't fight I will be a good boy," he says. "I won't do anything bad again."

Was the real issue about parental judgment? Doreen has concerns about the matches, but that is not the real issue. Rather, she is upset that they have been on vacation for nearly a week and Alfred hasn't approached her romantically. Just before she left the table to go to the ladies' room she noticed a couple holding hands and flirting with each other. This set her off. The issue of the matches became a convenient deflection for the hurt and rejection she felt. Instead of talking to her husband directly about these feelings, she expressed her distress in a "safer" manner.

What if Doreen had spoken to her husband about the feelings of rejection she experienced on their vacation and his response was less than supportive? She would have felt he added insult to her injury. This is not a pleasant feeling, especially when the issue under discussion creates a sense of vulnerability. And this is not uncommon; most of us have had the experience of putting forth a sensitive feeling only to be rebuffed. The result is that the temptation to play it safe and go *around* these experiences rather than confronting them directly becomes compelling. It can be so compelling that neither partner is able to sort out the real issue under the camouflage.

But as long as parents give in to this temptation to play it safe, it remains a short-term solution with long-term negative consequences. The child is drawn into the adult issues and usually becomes confused, anxious, and worse. The adults are avoiding their own issues, which not only limit them and their own growth but also impose limitations on the intimacy of their relationship. It is as if the kitchen is on fire and they are pouring water on the hallway.

Sometimes, the child is pulled into the adult relationship by one parent as a way to "get back" at the other parent. Perhaps the parent feels hurt or angry but doesn't know how to express this feeling directly. Consider yet another convoluted family drama. The scene is a tastefully furnished middle-class home in a quiet, tree-lined suburban neighborhood. In one variation or another, the clash about to take place has been reenacted innumerable times. Mary Jackson has just returned home from shopping on a Saturday afternoon. Her children had been told to do the dishes in her absence. As she drives up to her house, she honks the horn, but nobody comes out to help with the groceries. Annoyed, she goes inside with one of the heavy shopping bags.

There are dishes everywhere. The kitchen is a mess; nothing has been touched. Furious, she races upstairs, shuts off the blaring television set, and angrily confronts her two children, ages ten and twelve. She yells, "What is the meaning of this? How could you be so inconsiderate?"

At this moment, her husband, who was reading his newspaper in the backyard, appears. His wife is fuming and reprimands him for not supervising the children. She then demands that he speak to them. He agrees, but in doing so, he allows the children to see that he is condescending to their mother. He implies, "My heart isn't really in this, but I'd better say these things to get your mother off our backs." In admonishing the children, he manages to uphold his image as fellow victim and adds to his wife's image as villain.

The Jacksons thought they were focusing on parental authority, but this proved to be a superficial issue masking a more intimate one. Mr. Jackson was hurt that Mrs. Jackson spoke to her mother twice a day and seemed to confide more in her than she did in him. Mrs. Jackson was angry because she felt her husband was not emotionally available to her in the way her mother was. The children had become so accustomed to the double messages between their parents that they took full advantage and typically played up their role as "innocent" victims to avoid their responsibilities.

The drama in the Jackson household involves the role of victim and villain. The roles are interchangeable; husband, wife, and children are all eligible and have played both roles with equal facility. In the end, however, all fall victim to the effects of the camouflaged marital discord. Mrs. Jackson complains of frequent headaches, which her doctors have suggested are the result of tension. Mr. Jackson has high blood pressure that is exasperated by stress. Linda, the twelve-year-old, is failing academically, and Michael, her younger brother, frequently wets his bed.

In yet another version of the endless ways that children are drawn into adult issues as human shields, a child may be swayed to one parent's side in an effort to divert the other parent. Sally is a high-level executive for a womens'-wear manufacturer. She travels a good deal, and her husband, Mel, resents her being more successful than he is. He is not open about this; instead, he broods and hides his feelings. As a strategy against her, Mel begins to pamper their only child, whom he wishes to alienate from Sally in order to distract her from her career ambitions.

MEL: (disgusted) *You're not doing your job. Jeremy is being neglected.*

SALLY: (angry) *You're crazy!*

MEL: (self-righteously) *What do you mean crazy? You're never around to take care of him. You're always running off.*

SALLY: (insistent) *Jeremy gets excellent care. Since when did you become father of the year?*

MEL: (accusing) *How many nights have you been gone? The baby wakes up, and I have to take him into our bed!*

SALLY: (counterattacking) *What the hell are you taking a five-year-old into our bed for? Jeremy is well aware of my job and shouldn't ordinarily have any difficulty with it. Are you forgetting the times he has come to work with me and gone on trips with me? What about that? What about the time I spent with him explaining how I always come back? What are you trying to create?*

MEL: (angry) *I don't like it, goddamn it!*

SALLY: (crying) *That's it! I can't take your accusations and put-downs. It's hard enough trying to be everything to everyone. Without support, it is impossible.*

Eventually, Mel's destructive strategy succeeded to the point where Jeremy started recoiling from his mother when she returned from her business trips. Sally and Mel were divorced a year later.

It is quite clear that there are many ways parents can purposefully or unwittingly use a child to divert attention from or to camouflage the real issue: *the conflict between the parents.* By using their children in this destructive manner, parents invariably harm their children emotionally, often beyond repair. Children may begin to exhibit emotional, physical, behavioral, or academic difficulties that are a *direct* result of the stress created by forced inclusion in their parents' marital disharmony.

Many a parent has taken his or her child to a therapist with the hope that the therapist will "fix" the child's anger, depression, acting out, apparent school difficulty, or even a physical problem such as asthma, headaches, or stomach problems. And these parents are often surprised, disbelieving, or insulted when they find out that the cause of their child's problem comes not from an intrinsic problem with the child, but rather from the parents' difficulties that are not being addressed. Jim and Martha's fight about disciplining their children that turns out not to be about their children at all provides an example:

MARTHA: *You're too soft on the kids. You can't just let them do whatever they want.*

JIM: *I don't know what you're talking about. I simply told Bobby I'd rather he didn't go over to his friend's house. I didn't insist, and he decided to go anyway. Is that a crime?*

MARTHA: *That's not the point. It's because you didn't insist that I have to take all the responsibility for the kids. Who disciplines them? Me!*

JIM: *I don't agree. I do my part. What the hell is bugging you?*

MARTHA: (angrily) *I do all the dirty work! You prance through life without a care in the world. What is this? If you're not going to be home half the time, the least you can do is face up to your responsibilities when you're here . . .*

JIM: (interrupting) *You're angry because the kids and I have such a good relationship. You're always trying to make me the heavy.*

MARTHA: *Oh, bull!*

JIM: *Listen. I take enough responsibility trying to earn a living. I think I deal with the kids just fine.*

MARTHA: *How do you know how well you deal with them? You hardly see them, and they are having all kinds of problems. It all falls on me. I think they should see a child psychologist.*

JIM: *I don't think that's necessary, but if you feel strongly about it, it's OK with me.*

Jim and Martha were focusing on doing a good job of raising the kids, the role of the "man of the house," and discipline, but these proved to be sidetracks to other issues that neither dared confront. After meeting the parents and the children, the child psychologist suggested they consult with a couple therapist. It emerged that Martha felt left out of Jim's life—unattended, unattractive, and jealous of the time he devoted to his work. When Jim and Martha sought couple therapy, Martha learned to level about her real feelings, wants, and expectations. The issue of disciplining the children was never raised again.

What's Really Bugging You?

It is evident that many relationships come to resemble chronic-complaint departments. The same problems are aired repeatedly to no avail. And, as we've seen, oftentimes it is not even clear what the real issues are. The issue may be suppressed, camouflaged, or put forth abruptly, defensively, vaguely, in the form of a lecture, or with substantial hostility. On the surface, clearly defining the issues sounds absurdly easy, and for some few people it is. For many, though, going beyond the basics—he frequently leaves clothes around; she forgets to gas up the car; he hogs the newspaper; she monopolizes conversations—isn't as easy as it seems.

Even if the children are not used as "decoys," it is not uncommon, for instance, to find that the apparent focus rests on an insignificant issue, while the actual issue is related to something entirely different. A man may nag a woman for being a mediocre housekeeper (even though the housekeeping is only a mild irritant at most) because he is jealous of her winning personality and her close friendships. His struggle to make friends and be liked has been less than spectacular, and he assumes that attacking her on her popularity will expose his own feelings of inadequacy and envy. In order to avoid this painful self-disclosure, he chooses (perhaps without being aware of it) to pick on something safe for him, his partner's housekeeping. In effect, he is saying, "See, you aren't so terrific after all," without having to risk revealing himself.

Consider Mr. and Mrs. Smith, a couple who argue regularly about his coming to dinner on time. Mrs. Smith describes the problem quite simply: "My husband is always late for dinner. That's all there is to it." Prompted to discuss the specific sequence of events prior to the dinner hour, Mrs. Smith broadened the perspective.

At six o'clock, when my husband arrives home, I am in the kitchen putting the finishing touches on dinner. At six fifteen, after washing up and changing his clothes, my husband brings me a whiskey sour and a beer for himself, and we take ten minutes out for a drink. There is usually some pleasant talk of the day's happenings, and my husband usually gets himself another beer. Typically, I suggest he give me a hand in the kitchen rather than finishing his second drink alone. And, typically, he grumbles about my suggestion while I go back into the kitchen muttering some angry thoughts about equality and all that stuff.

Then comes six forty-five. Dinner's ready and on the table. I call once—no answer. Twice. "Yeah, I'm coming." Five minutes later I go into the TV room enraged and tell him that dinner's cold and he's an inconsiderate bastard.

Now he comes. We eat in silence; we don't even exchange glances. After dinner we soften; he even helps with the dishes occasionally. That is our dinner routine.

Looking at the more detailed pattern, it is evident the problem involves more than remedying a simple case of tardiness. Mrs. Smith acknowledges that beckoning her husband repeatedly doesn't work, yet she plays her part in the dinnertime drama in exactly the same manner each evening. How is it that Mrs. Smith doesn't tire of being rejected in her bid for help? And couldn't Mrs. Smith call her husband several minutes before dinner was ready? Certainly, this seems an obvious solution. How did she miss it? Is there some sort of payoff Mr. and Mrs. Smith derive from their behavior?

Scrutinizing her actions, Mrs. Smith realizes that, in fact, she does not want her husband's help in the kitchen even though she requests it on cue each evening. This becomes apparent when Mrs. Smith asks herself what she wants her husband to do in the kitchen. In actuality, she would rather do everything herself. By asking her husband to help out, Mrs. Smith is really fishing for a statement of appreciation for her *own* efforts. Reluctantly, Mrs. Smith also recognizes that her husband's rejection affords her the opportunity to feel "one up" by badgering him about his uncooperativeness.

While his wife bemoans her fate, Mr. Smith expresses his resentment and wrestles out of his "one down" position through noncompliance: "Let her call me; it serves her right for asking me to help after a hard day's work. I'll show her who's in charge here." The dinnertime dilemma is now redefined. Mrs. Smith wants to feel appreciated and respected; Mr. Smith wants the same. The evening meal simply became a convenient—and misleading—arena.

Some couples report a pattern of fights that break out over something quite obviously trivial after their lovemaking has been particularly satisfying and connective. Unlike the Smiths, or even couples who draw their children in as shields, these couples keep love at bay to avoid the feeling of engulfment. Typically, this is an adult who, as a child, was not allowed to satisfy a natural need for independence and now mistrusts anything (like closeness) that hints at restraint.

It works this way: one of them complains about the other's annoying habit, or some minor frustration gives rise to a disproportionate reaction, or the kids are too noisy and a volley of accusations results. It could be any number of imperfections in living arrangements, and there is no dearth of these to complain about for people whose lives are intertwined. In any case, one person gets furious, and the other one is ignited and becomes enraged. In a flash, harsh words are exchanged and the recent lovemaking seems like a distant memory.

And that is just the point. Some fights have no issue except, "Keep your distance!" It is reminiscent of the porcupine story referred to earlier. Some love partners who find themselves fighting about things that seem not worth the effort may have unconsciously designed the fight to create distance without making the other partner feel rejected or having to face their own fears of closeness.

Last, most of us are prone to hide what we want behind the guise of right and wrong. This is an underlying attitude that, if held, stymies even the best intentions of couples who are struggling with discord. In fact, proclamations of right and wrong are usually arbitrary rules that an individual assigns to his or her preferences. A man, for example, is lying on the couch on a Sunday afternoon watching the football game. His partner attacks him: "How can you lie there all day? Only an idiot would spend his Sunday in front of the TV!" The man rushes to his defense: "This is my only chance to relax! Look who's talking anyway, you with your ridiculous craft projects!" The implication here is that there is something the matter with the man—he is doing something wrong, something he should feel guilty about. His response is, in effect, "I'm OK; there's something wrong with you." The wrong-begets-wrong cycle is likely to escalate as both parties become further entrenched in their own truth. Thus, the discussion becomes adversarial and fixed on who's right and who's wrong. In actuality, the issue, as with most, is based less on right and wrong than on preference: "I like/I don't like; I want/I don't want." In this instance, the wife wanted to spend some time with her husband on a Sunday afternoon, and instead of stating that directly, she protected her feelings from rejection by attacking him instead. She hoped that by her "there's something wrong with you" message she could provoke him into shutting off the TV and paying attention to her without having to reveal her desire directly.

Guidelines for Authentic Fighting

We have seen that while all couples fight, at least occasionally, it is very easy to fight dishonestly. That is, the real issues remain untouched while the emotions roar and the words fly, all in the wrong direction. Here are several suggestions for the good fight, or better yet, a discussion that isn't shadowed by overwrought emotion.

- If your partner has accused you of being defensive, or if you realize that about yourself, make an effort not to block off the feelings hidden *behind* your usual reactions. Instead, reflect on the feelings that are hiding beneath. As you open to greater understanding of yourself, you need to risk sharing this with your partner, with the understanding that this sharing is a sacred trust that is not to be violated. This means not using a disclosure to shame or chastise a partner and keeping the disclosure confidential. If this confidence is maintained, you will gradually begin to view your partner's emotional concerns as well as your own with more compassion. It may seem as if simply talking about your feelings is insufficient. However, the combination of increased awareness and talking out your feelings is truly a dramatic change from past patterns. What's more, when the feelings underlying relationship dissatisfaction are expressed in an honest, responsible manner, it is far more likely that the listener will be responsive.

- Couples that find themselves in unproductive disputes often find that they are *reactive* with each other. People are the most reactive when they feel emotionally threatened or provoked. Frequently the feelings that arise are far out of proportion to the events that evoked them. When you are reactive, you say things such as: "Every time my wife (husband) offers one of her (his) 'suggestions,' I can feel the anger erupting in me." "She (he) really knows how to get to me. Sometimes just being around him (her) gets me tense." "I can't believe that nothing I do ever gets a positive response. I don't know why it still upsets me."

The opposite of being reactive is being *responsive*. When you are responsive, you are aware of your feelings but don't let them run you. This is extremely empowering. Responsiveness allows you to maintain some control in the face of the competing thoughts and feelings of your partner. You will open all sorts of new options and choices in dealing with each other, because your perspective and your sense of reason aren't being blurred by emotion. Feeling more in control, you will be in a better position to take control of your love life.

Of course, becoming responsive is easier said than done; it requires that you identify what it is that you want, believe, or feel—and stay your course. It also involves being open to views that are in conflict with yours, rather than getting defensive. In talking to your partner, for example, instead of arguing ferociously or explaining yourself frantically, you might simply listen carefully without interrupting (a dead giveaway that you are being reactive) and say something like, "I understand what you are saying; your view is credible, but I see it differently." Or, rather than react emotionally, you might say, "I am viewing things differently; let me think about it a bit and then we'll discuss it."

- A law of physics states that every action has an equal and opposing reaction; correspondingly, every issue is an interaction between *two* people. For example, there can be no dominating husband without a submissive wife, no interrupting wife without a passive and willing husband. Every "villain" requires a cooperative "victim." Consequently, when discussing a problem, it is good policy to state your *own* role in the issue as well as your view of your partner's. If you are interested in promoting openness, it is best to start with yourself.

Here are some additional suggestions that will prepare you for fine-tuning your discussions and creating even more openness:

- Compose a list of the major criticisms you have about your partner. Now, sit down facing your spouse and reverse roles. Take turns speaking *as if you were your partner*, and express his or her feelings about one of the items on your list. Get into the role and present as thorough an understanding of this issue as possible *from your partner's point of view*. For example, a husband playing his wife might take an item (she falls asleep too early, for instance) from his list of complaints about her and say, "I'm really tired after a full day's work, cooking dinner, and putting the children to bed. I know you get annoyed if I fall asleep early, so I try my best to stay up. Sometimes, though, I'm so exhausted I just can't make it." Try to really get into the experience of being your partner and understanding things from his or her viewpoint. Continue alternating until each of the criticism lists has been completed.

The ability to be compassionate toward a partner begins with attempting to understand him or her. Take at least half an hour to discuss your experience of this. What did you learn about your partner? About yourself? See if you can get into passionately defending your partner's (as well as your own) right to be fallible. Remind yourself of this acceptance equation when you are feeling intolerant of your partner: being human = being fallible.

- Human beings are great "should makers." We are sufficiently egotistical to believe that because we would prefer something to occur, it *should* occur. The behaviors we view as more desirable in our partner *should* replace those deemed less desirable. Seldom do we stop to think, "Whoever guaranteed us that the world (our world, our family members) was designed to conform to our demands?" In the following acceptance experience, we will increase our awareness of the absurdity of the "should" rule.

Take turns beginning a sentence with "You should _____" and complete the statement with the demand that your spouse be different. For example, "You should be neater." It is very important that as you express your "should," you take the role of a parent scolding a child. Raise your voice, talk down to your partner—literally, by standing up and hovering over him or her, pointing your finger, and scowling. Do you feel somewhat like a nagging parent with your spouse? Now face each other, make good eye contact, and touch each other. Say the following sentence to each other, and pause to absorb what you experience as you do this: "I may not like some of your behaviors, but I value you overall."

- Sadly, many of us are caught up in negativism—so much that we are more alert to unpleasant occurrences than to pleasant ones. Some positive occurrences are taken for granted, some are minimized or even misunderstood, and occasionally some are silently noted. Too infrequently we express appreciation. It is likely that most of us would like to hear statements of appreciation more often—the objective of this last experience.

Sit facing your partner, and take turns beginning a sentence with "I appreciate _____" and go on to state your appreciation in sufficient detail so that your partner has a good sense of what it is that you find pleasing. Take about five minutes to do this. If you get stuck, just begin the sentence "I appreciate _____," maintain good eye contact with your partner, and see what words come to you. Allow ample time to discuss how you felt as you gave and received appreciation. Be sure to include in your discussion the topic, "how I can bring my appreciation of you into our daily living." Conclude the discussion when both of you have offered at least one viable suggestion for increasing expressions of appreciation.

A caveat: because some of these suggestions are to be called upon during the heat of confrontation, when emotional arousal is sure to be high, they have to be overlearned if they are to be accessible when most needed.

9

THE EMOTIONAL
CONFERENCE

In order to become more intimate, we must reveal our deepest feelings to each other. Unlike the experience of childhood, in marriage we have an opportunity to be who we truly are rather than conform to someone else's vision of what we "should" be. The key question is whether we feel our true self, nakedly revealed, will be found acceptable.

We all need opportunities to let our hair down—to be weak, to be sad, to be childish, to be crazy—sometimes, somewhere, with someone. That place is at home, with an intimate. A sound relationship permits a range of expressions from anger to affection without fear of condemnation. Thus, we can be as we really are: weak when we feel weak, scared when we feel confused, childish when the responsibilities of adulthood become overwhelming. Relationships that cease to provide sanctuary are those in which weaknesses are used as weapons, so that acting "out-of-character" is quickly suppressed.

Take Pam and Arnold, a couple living very traditionally. Arnold doesn't acknowledge Pam's existence unless she behaves in a certain way.

The desired behavior is not clearly defined, although Pam knows that what Arnold wants—"an understanding housewife who is efficient and charming"—isn't always how she feels. When Pam insists on being herself, which is sometimes needy, inefficient, and not so charming, she is told by Arnold, "You're mistaken. You're not the way you think you are. I know you. Deep inside you really are an undemanding housewife."

In some instances, the tactics of nonacceptance go beyond denying or discounting part of an intimate's being and take the form of a direct attack at a sensitive area. Nina and Don are both in their early thirties and have been married for eight years. Nina is pregnant with their second child, and they are planning to move from their apartment into a house. Don is hard working and earnest; however, as a young consulting engineer with very little business experience, he has suffered some serious financial setbacks.

NINA: *That house in Lakeside is perfect for us. The location is first-class—we'll be making a great investment.*

DON: *It does have lots of nice qualities, but I'm afraid that the asking price, combined with the large mortgage we'd have to carry, makes it out of reach for us.*

NINA: *Well, have you seen something that is more affordable?*

DON: *Yes, the houses in Davisport are larger, the taxes are lower, and the prices are within reason.*

NINA: *Are you kidding? That area is nowhere. Who would want to live there?*

DON: *What do you mean? We both grew up there. It's a solid, stable, middle-class area with good schools and services.*

NINA: (beginning the attack) *We could have afforded the house in Lakeside if your consulting firm hadn't collapsed.*

DON: *That was my first attempt in a business venture . . .*

NINA: *Yes, and it failed. Now you seem to have given up. Working for someone else isn't going to produce any real money. If you had listened to me, maybe things wouldn't have gone sour and we would have the money.*

DON: *I admit I made some bad decisions; that's why I am learning more about the business.*

NINA: *Bad decisions? Hell, you couldn't even hold a business together, and now you tell me you can't even provide a nice home for your family!*

DON: *Davisport homes are nice. . . .*

NINA: *Look, we're going to buy the house in Lakeside. I'll ask my father for the money. I'll explain to him how you can't handle buying the right house and that you're not a savvy businessman; he'll loan us enough for a large down payment, and you won't have to worry.*

DON: *Nina, you know it is important to me not to take money from your parents. You've done this before, disregarding my feelings; we'll take the house in Lakeside. I'll find a way to make it work.*

NINA: (having effectively crushed Don's self-regard) *I knew you would work it out. I'll call the real estate agent and make the arrangements.*

While most of us want to be loved and respected by our partners, we also fear that we may be found undesirable, as was just illustrated. For some, this fear of rejection leads us to go into hiding. We become guarded and cautious because we believe that exposure of real feelings will lead to being unwanted: "If my partner really got to know me, he (she) wouldn't want any part of me." Consequently, a good deal of the stress and strain of the human condition comes from our striving to be something we are not; many of us fail to accept ourselves as fallible and, therefore, far-from-perfect human beings. Likewise, our failure to accept our partners, warts and all, is a significant source of relationship distress.

In striking contrast to those who castigate their partners or make subtle (and sometimes harsh) judgments is the individual who is self-accepting and who consequently has the strength and understanding to tolerate the foibles of another. Matthew, a forty-eight-year-old high school English teacher, was fortunate to become involved with such an individual. He had been divorced three months when he met Helen, a woman with whom he developed a stormy but ultimately positive relationship.

When I met Helen, one of my strongest and most persistent feelings was pain—not just emotional pain but actual physical pain: nausea, headaches, and the like. I remember saying once that when my wife left me for another man and I lost the connection to my family, it was as if a knife were put into me and turned around each day to cut up my insides. My first reaction to Helen was one of surprise at her sensitivity and awareness of what I was feeling, even when I expressed it inarticulately or hardly at all. Then I began to get the feeling that not only was she sensitive but that she also cared about me. It seems crazy, but I fought desperately against this. I was firmly convinced that to give in to her acceptance of me meant selling my soul; there would be a high price for allowing another person into my life. Indeed, I was still reeling from the last time I yielded.

I tried demonstrating to her how unworthy I was—how selfish, inadequate, and nasty I could be. I tried hating and attacking her. I told her that she couldn't possibly think well of me, that I was defective. I suggested that she was being deceitful and cruel to pretend that she accepted me. But she was always there, treating me with respect; she was a firm, strong pillar that I beat on to no avail and that merely said, "You are a worthwhile human being." Not once was I able to draw her in and get her to be defensive. She saw past my game playing, yet she didn't condemn me for it. Not that she was a saint; she expressed anger, outrage, and frustration. She engaged me and fought ferociously, but she always did so in a way that didn't belittle me. Her words were strong yet soft; somehow the sharp edges were removed. She conveyed that I was not an obnoxious person but a person acting in an obnoxious manner at times. In other words, I was not disqualified and considered garbage because of my difficulties. Nor was I able to drag her down. This was a woman who knew who she was and was unwavering in her belief in herself. I had never experienced anything quite like that.

As I look back on it now, I was putting all my faults and inade-quacies on the line so that I could be done with the process of rejec-tion. And Helen calmly (and sometimes not so calmly), by her acceptance of me as a person, peeled off my armor layer by layer. Slowly, it became clear that I am the one who makes the ultimate judgment of my worth. That sounds like a simple, commonsense state-ment. Yet my appreciation of that dictum has given me such a sense of peace that it is awesome. I feel elevated, freer, accepting not only of myself but of others as well. In my relationships with other people, I try to see them as individuals struggling with the same issues as I do, not as adversaries or enemies. Most of us want the same things in our relationships: honesty, a sharing of feelings and thoughts, empathy, support, fun. Keeping these things in mind, my tolerance for others has expanded and my relationships, as a result, are much richer.

It should not be construed from the foregoing report by Matthew that acceptance is the same thing as liking. Obviously, we may not like all that another person is, but by acceptance we acknowledge that and respect the fact that he or she is worthwhile. It is this attitude that expresses, "I may not like some of your behavior patterns, but that doesn't make you less of a person." People willing to reach out to oth-ers with this attitude can accept and tolerate differences without con-demning the individual. They are wise to the human struggle and, consequently, when another person behaves negatively, an attempt is made to understand the basis of the action.

What's more, Helen did not put her energy into fixing Matthew; she realized that wasn't her job, nor is it possible to fix another person, even if you would like to do so. Aware of her own defenses, she was able to see through those of Matthew without feeling personally attacked. Helen knew who she was and was not about to let someone else define her. Matthew probably gained more from Helen having a strong sense of self than anything she could have said to him. Her accepting of herself grad-ually led to Matthew's becoming more willing to embrace himself. He began to understand that we are all a work in progress. Being accepted in this manner is something we can get, in varying degrees, only from our interpersonal relationships with wise parents, good friends, and some educators. It is endemic to some love relationships. And it is precisely this feeling of being accepted and valued that promotes openness with an intimate.

Emotional Conferencing

The relationship Matthew and Helen formed was stormy, but it was headed in the right direction. The right direction involves revealing ourselves beyond the roles and expectations we have assumed in our daily lives. As we deepen our ability to contact and respond authentically, we discover what it means to connect with another person. In those moments when we do meet with our love partner heart-to-heart, emotionally naked, we feel known and loved, accurately and fully, to a degree we seldom experience anywhere else in our lives. It would be terrific if we could increase those moments.

Toward that effort, some years ago I sought to develop a simple, brief, yet powerful experience a couple could provide for themselves that would create those heart-to-heart moments. Through experimenting and trying it in my own marriage (weekly, for two years), I developed the emotional conference. It is an opportunity for a couple to be open— fully and accurately—by expressing how each has been affected by their partner's behavior. The emotional conference consists of a fifteen-minute date for a meeting at the same time each week. The agenda is feelings and reflection on where the feelings have their roots.

Each partner spends five minutes talking about how the other's actions have affected him or her emotionally. The actions may have occurred at any time during the course of the relationship, all the way back to the first date. There is no statute of limitation. Interruption is not permitted. While one partner is speaking the other is listening, and each partner will mirror (that is, reflect back) what the other has said when he or she is finished. The two or three minutes of mirroring each partner (after they have each had five minutes to speak) accounts for the full fifteen minutes of the experience.

The speaker should begin by briefly describing the incident and then describing how he or she was emotionally affected. Further, if the speaker can relate his or her feelings to his or her upbringing ("I feel unsupported by you, just the way I felt growing up. My parents never had anything positive to say to me."), this will enrich the experience for both the speaker and listener.

It must be noted, this is *not* a gripe session; it is an intimacy builder. The speaker is talking about his or her own feelings. The listener is getting to know how his or her partner responds emotionally and more about his or her partner's vulnerability as well as the origin of sensitivities.

Consider it this way: when couples enter therapy to work out issues in their relationship, they are invariably focused on the other person's being the problem, and they see the other person's changing as the solution. What invariably happens is that no change occurs! The irony is that the only way we can move out of an impasse is to give up on directing our energy toward fixing the other person and to put our energy into working on ourselves—not only expressing what we are feeling and thinking, but discovering how we have come to be particularly sensitive about certain things.

The emotional conference directs the focus back on you and away from your partner. This does not mean, however, that we view ourselves as the cause of the problems or that taking the focus off our partner implies that we withdraw or distance ourselves. Rather, it means that we become better able to share our own perspective, to state clearly our own views and feelings, and to reveal who we are underneath the protective armor. It is an opportunity to begin the challenging self-exploration that is necessary for a deep and nourishing connection with a love partner. Of course, the goal is not just to move toward connectedness—meaning *any* kind of connectedness. Rather, the challenge is to move toward a connectedness that preserves and appreciates the individuality of each partner, allowing for real intimacy. These are the few simple rules of the emotional conference:

- Use "I" statements. You are talking about your feelings, not casting blame on the other person. Briefly describe what happened, and then express your feelings. Then reveal what you think you contributed to the incident. The incident might have been a minor thing or some major blowup. The incident or issue (it doesn't have to stem from a particular incident or behavior) can also be something positive that has moved you; it doesn't necessarily have to be negative. What is essential is that you spend time before the conference thinking about the feelings involved and whether or not the feelings are familiar—that is, feelings you experienced as a child.
- Absolutely no interruptions are allowed. One person speaks; the other listens. No exceptions.
- After the speaker is done, the listener summarizes the major points without editing, analyzing, interpreting, or judging. When both partners have spoken and mirrored each other, the experience is completed. There is no further discussion of what was said.
- Each person should have a separate agenda. The second partner doesn't get to rebut what the first person said. Otherwise the conference degenerates into one asking, "How could you see it that way?" and the other countering, "Why don't you see it the way I do?" And that is just what you want to avoid! All too often, love partners insist that they share the same point of view, and this is what leads them into fruitless argument. Being different people, it follows that we will sometimes have a different view of the same events. Insisting otherwise is a prescription for unhappiness. Real intimacy requires a profound respect for differences. Don't make the mistake of confusing closeness with sameness and behaving as if you and your partner should share a common brain.

What is the point of the emotional conference? It is hoped that both partners will consider how their actions affect each other, learn to listen attentively, and reveal themselves, vulnerability and all. The experience is more than a weekly reminder that no two people, even the long and happily married, view incidents and actions in exactly the same way. It provides an opportunity to take responsibility for your own feelings and to reflect on how your feelings link to experiences with your family of origin—the family you came from. Let's look at an example of a couple going through the conference experience:

Andy, thirty-nine, and Ruth, thirty-four, had been in a relationship for eight years and found that they were fighting nearly every time they were together and that their fights were instigated by things that barely made sense to them. The fights involved Ruth's complaints about the lack of time spent together and included Andy's not calling when promised, working too late, reading at the kitchen table, and not answering her page.

Andy's arguments involved his contempt for Ruth's complaints about him. He took every opportunity to point out to Ruth that she had become dependent and unable to take care of herself—he often became infuriated at her for minor "infractions" like driving the car low on gas and forgetting to buy something at the market. Ruth countered that Andy was confusing her desire to be with him with an inability to take care of herself. "You act like you don't like me," she told him with tears in her eyes. "I can't remember the last time you had something nice to say to me. All I hear is you being defensive and never admitting to anything. It seems I am always wrong in your eyes."

"And you have made me too important in your life," Andy snapped. "I feel smothered by you. I never get any time for myself. I am either working or with you, getting blamed for the time I am not with you. I can't stand it anymore. Get a life!"

Like most of their adversarial exchanges, the words they threw back and forth at each other became increasingly harsh until they both felt demoralized about the prospects of ever recapturing the happiness they once shared.

Here is a glimpse at their backgrounds: Andy's mother struggled with depression all during his childhood. Every problem his mother had somehow became his father's fault. His mother seemed to hate his father, and, consequently, she often confided in Andy and turned to him for comfort. The pressure he felt from his mother to "fill in" for his father had caused him to be resentful and influenced him to keep busy as a way to escape from her. He felt the responsibility for his mother's feelings had fallen from his father to him.

Ruth recalled her parents' being so disorganized and so heavily embroiled in conflict with each other that they had little time or energy to pay attention to her. She rarely had any special time with her parents, especially her father, an aspiring inventor. Her father spent futile months huddled in the basement with each new project that he dreamed was going to bring him fame and fortune. Ruth never felt important to him. While she acknowledged that her childhood household had had many positive elements, the pain of rejection is what she remembered and felt most sharply.

Andy and Ruth began their first experience with the emotional conference hopefully, but it was not long before they had regressed to their familiar pattern. Each of them thought that the other was at fault for the conference not going well. Andy was convinced that Ruth had misunderstood the directions; Ruth was absolutely certain that she was correct and he was wrong. Furthermore, she felt she had taken responsibility for the conference's occurring. She resented Andy for putting it off until the last minute, not giving it (and her) priority.

In the early weeks of the emotional conference, they continually interrupted each other, challenged each other's "inaccuracies," and began "innocent" discussion afterward that erupted into arguments. Both of them were discouraged, and they wanted to discontinue doing the conference. Something, however, kept them at it. Perhaps it was the feeling that if they could only stick to the guidelines it would go better and help them heal the emotional pain both of them felt. And that is what happened. It was four months later, in the weekly conference. Andy went first; looking directly at Ruth, he said the following:

When you took a car trip out West a few years ago, the thought occurred to me that I wished you would have a fatal accident so I would be free. I wouldn't be a "shit" that abandoned you; I would be the poor guy who lost his love. A dark seed took root in my mind at that time. As irra-

tional as it is, a profoundly disturbing idea haunts me: on the day that thought blinked to life in my head, I had turned bad. I was tested and found wanting. My rational mind tells me lots of couples struggling with each other have such thoughts. The thoughts come out of desperation, not out of evil. But my heart says otherwise. Since that day, I have been troubled by a primitive suspicion that in some cosmic account book, in some dusty ledger of karmic debts and credits, your unhappiness is being charged to my account. I feel guilty and have often found myself barely able to look you in the eye. Every opportunity I have to avoid you, I take. It is not because I dislike you or that I don't love you. It is because of my own feelings of not feeling that I live up to what you want me to be. I feel guilty because I know you are a good person despite the differences between us. And now I realize that I bring to our differences my own issues with my mother, and I have taken out my anger on you instead of placing it where it belongs.

Ruth sat quietly and listened. She had tears running down her face, and Andy looked as if he were straining to avoid becoming teary as well. She was apparently very moved by what Andy had said, but she neither offered comfort nor editorialized. She took in a deep breath and went on for about two minutes or so to summarize what Andy said in demonstration of her understanding. In essence, she told Andy that she heard him say that inherent in the anger he had toward her was the demand he felt made on him as a child by his mother: "Take care of me; I am your responsibility." His view of her left him feeling helpless, just like he felt with his mother. He had felt so helpless that he wished Ruth would not be around anymore and that he was not responsible for that—and he felt like a bad person for having that wish. In fact, he had felt responsible and guilty that he was not making her happy, and he avoided her because being around her made him feel bad. Andy nodded in acknowledgement, and then Ruth took her turn:

If I were to reduce all my feelings and their painful conflicts to a single name, I can think of no other word but shame. *It was shame— shame and insecurity—that I felt in all those hours in pursuit of my father for the simplest recognition. Getting a "Hello" when he came in the door would have been a start. I felt ashamed by my neediness, shamed by the hunger in my soul that I considered forbidden and weak. I thought I had gotten over that by the time I met you, and I believed you were different and it would be different between us. I am not happy about how I've acted with you. My hunger triggered the same pattern of chasing after you that I had done with my father. And the rejection I felt was the same experience I had with my father, making it all the more painful. I don't think it is fair for me to expect you to make up for the neglect of my father. I realize that the more I wanted from you and the more intense I became about it, the more it pushed you away. Rather than stepping back and seeing that, I became angry and more aggressive. That was a mistake for myself as well as for you, and I regret it.*

As Ruth had done, Andy sat quietly, kept his eyes on her, and listened carefully. The images that had floated before his and Ruth's eyes—particularly the emotional wounds of their childhood that had been playing out in their marriage—were not comforting. Rather than thinking his own thoughts while Ruth spoke, as he had done when they first started doing the conference, he did his best to focus on her words and the meaning they had for her. When her statement was completed, he "mirrored" back what she said, as she had done for him. In essence, he told her, "You feel ashamed about feeling needy—feeling that helplessness you felt as a child chasing your father for attention. You don't like how that feels. Buried in your criticism of me is your wound from childhood. You have been saying to me in a variety of ways: 'Why can't you make me feel as if I count? The way you view me makes me feel invisible and I want to be seen.' You regret feeling so insignificant in relation to me and don't want to continue giving me responsibility for how you feel."

Here is Andy's reaction to the conferences:

Although that particular conference was a turning point, it didn't occur until after we had been doing the conference for some time. It took us a while before we felt safe enough with each other to really be deeply open. In fact, while we were driving one day, after we had only done the conference a few times, I was thinking about really being honest about my feelings. I turned to Ruth and asked her to promise not to bring up anything I say in the conference and use it against me. She readily agreed and then asked me to promise the same. I did. Despite the promises, we were both pretty frazzled some evenings after the conference. It wasn't easy hearing what the other person said and not reacting. I confess that there were some nights I was talking to Ruth for a few hours about what she said—talking to her in my head, not directly to her. Now all that inner chatter has quieted down. And I am happy to say that we now look forward to Wednesday evening, the night we do the conference.

Here is Ruth's reaction:

The conferences didn't have an immediate impact on our relationship, but slowly they brought us closer. Our bickering eventually just decreased and then it stopped. Both of us became more relaxed, more open and secure about our commitment. For a long time I experienced a sense of relief as a result of being able to talk openly without fear of fighting or reprisal, but I was also frightened and embarrassed. We both felt a little foolish that in all the years we've been together, the issues we've uncovered—about the unfinished business of our childhood—should have been obvious, but neither of us made the connection before.

Now that we have been doing it for nearly eight months, we find that we interact with each other differently at other times as well. Rather than interrupting or preparing a rebuttal when the other person is speaking, we really listen and try to understand. It has helped us to recognize our differences as people without insisting that we feel and think the same about things. We both realize that we have different sensitivities and that it is important to respect that. Andy doesn't have to respond to the same things in the same way I do, and he gives me the same respect. Coming to terms with that has been very helpful. Initially we both found ways to have a discussion of what was said so that we could have the opportunity to influence the other's viewpoint.

We eventually stopped doing that. Now we hear each other and mir-
ror, but we don't discuss what was said at all. It provides a good oppor-
tunity to "contain" the other's feelings without diluting them.

"Containing" the other's feelings, as Ruth puts it, gives each partner the opportunity to accept that he or she does not and cannot control how other people think about you. Because most of us have not
fully grown out of the childhood state of needing the approval of others in order to feel good about ourselves, taking in another's view of our
behavior without seeking to "correct" it is a valuable experience. Having a stable sense of "I" that is based primarily on self-validation rather
than other-validation allows love partners to navigate the delicate balance between separateness and connectedness. In effect, if each partner has a solid sense of "I," it is easier to form the "we" in a relationship.

At the simplest level, having a solid sense of "I" means that we can
be who we are in a relationship rather than what others' wish, need, and
expect us to be. It also means that we can allow others to do the same.
A solid sense of self allows you to use the emotional conference to do
the following:

- Present a balanced view of your strengths and vulnerabil-
  ities as well as what you've noticed yourself doing to avoid
  facing yourself.
- Make clear and honest statements that reflect your beliefs
  and experiences, past and present. This means that you are
  willing and able to reflect on how your upbringing has
  influenced your current relationship.
- Stay emotionally connected with your significant other,
  even (and especially) when things become emotionally
  intense.
- Address real (and perhaps painful) issues with your partner,
  not the pseudo issues that sometimes are used to
  camouflage what really matters.

The emotional conference is a powerful tool that can contribute to
the process of strengthening the "I" and repairing the sense of "we." It

is deceptively straightforward, and if it is done conscientiously, it will prompt you to take time from a busy day to focus on your feelings and the emotional patterns of your family of origin. It should occur once a week, but in circumstances where the issues have accumulated over time, doing it more often may be warranted.

Self-Soothing

The experience of being open and vulnerable, not only through what you say but in what you hear your partner say as occurs in the emotional conference, is not easy. Over time, doing the emotional conference will provide you with a more accurate picture of yourself and your love relationship. If you are bringing in the links to your family of origin, you will become increasingly aware of how your family imprinted you with a relationship blueprint that is being lived out with your partner. Your heightened awareness may be accompanied by strong emotions that need to be soothed. Confronting yourself through your own reflection and expression as well as through the eyes of your love partner will almost certainly call on you to draw from your inner resources. No one is without vulnerability, anxieties, and problems.

The most important principle of growing, and this applies whether or not the relationship is supportive, is self-empowerment. Each of us is in charge of our own growth. Taking charge involves turning inward and accessing your own resources to steady your emotional balance. This is called self-soothing, your ability to be in control of your emotions, to comfort and care for yourself without excessive indulgence. It is the process of putting what is going on with you—the change and growth, which can be frightening—into perspective.

Indeed, managing our emotions is something of a full-time job. Much of what we do—from reading fiction or watching TV to choosing friends—is in the service of making ourselves feel better. The ability to soothe ourselves is a fundamental life skill; most of us in the psychological professions view self-soothing as one of the most essential psychic tools. In fact, it is difficult to envision being able to survive without the ability to withstand the emotional storms that are part of a deep love relationship.

Self-soothing does not involve overindulgence, emotional regression, or food or substance bingeing. It does involve taking care of yourself while you're stretching the boundaries of openness and honesty with your partner. Self-soothing permits you to quiet and calm yourself; it is self-care but not self-indulgence. The process requires that you not give up on yourself or tell yourself it is too hard to settle your emotions down. It may be difficult, but you have to stick with yourself, just as you would with a friend going through a difficult time. Here are some specific suggestions for soothing yourself:

- If you are having a hard time—especially if you are uncovering painful issues from your family of origin—as much as practically possible, reduce the number and complexity of tasks confronting you by notifying those around you, including your children, to temporarily make fewer demands. Work-related projects and extra responsibilities (e.g., volunteer activities), which add to a hectic, pressured schedule, should be postponed for the time being. In a sense, an ailing psyche, like an ailing body, requires special attention and energy until it is strengthened.
- You may have to break off or reduce contact with your partner to self-repair when the exchange between you and your partner is consistently too unsettling. At the very least, attempt to do less together and enjoy it more rather than the reverse. The duration and degree of physical separation are determined by your emotional state: how badly you are feeling and how quickly you can recover from contact. Make it clear to your partner that your time-out is for self-repair, not withdrawal. Once replenished, you are in a better position to renew your efforts to regain connection with your partner.
- Do your best to stop the negative mental tapes. Stop "awfulizing" the situation and asking yourself, "How could he (or she)

feel this way?" Accept the present reality and settle down. Quiet yourself instead of exacerbating your very emotional state and losing perspective.

- To help regulate your emotions, look at your history and recall challenges that you faced successfully. Remind yourself that you are resilient. If you can't regulate your emotions, control your behavior. Once again, try to regain some perspective; reactions and situations don't last forever. Behave in a productive manner that you'll respect afterward, even if your emotions suggest otherwise. In other words, ask yourself, "If I felt better, how would I handle this?" Then, do your best to at least approximate that behavior. In contrast, when you start saying, "Maybe I shouldn't do that, but . . ." or "Maybe I shouldn't say that but . . ." take your own advice.

- If doing the emotional conference brings up a lot of family issues, as it did for Ruth and Andy, one of the most effective things you can do to release your emotional pain is to write about it. Set aside some time, and write letters to everyone in your family whom you feel hurt you or let you down. No one needs to see these letters but you, so don't hold back, censor yourself, or worry about how well the letter is written. Just put all the hurt and rage that's been festering inside and contaminating your system on the page. You may also want to write a letter to yourself. An important aspect of self-soothing is to stop punishing yourself for past mistakes. Instead, write a letter of forgiveness. Look back at regrettable actions; recall who you were at the time. Remind yourself that you are a work in progress, ever evolving, always learning, and fallible. Perfection isn't for human beings.

- In addition to providing a safe and effective medium for expressing yourself by using the emotional conference, create a peaceful place inside you. If you can tap that source, you can stop distress from building up, allowing your mind to clear and focus more sharply. There are numerous ways to cre-

ate calm: yoga, meditation, a walk in nature, a hot aromatic
bath, a good massage, soothing music, prayer, deep breathing, pleasant memories, and so on.

Do not expect these suggestions to be easily or quickly soothing.
When the wound is deep, the greatest trap is to expect too much heal-
ing to happen too soon. Particularly during a period when the hurt is
acute, it is wise to fortify yourself on the nourishment that friends and
individual interests provide.

10

BEYOND WORDS

SEX AND INTIMACY

Sexuality does not ordinarily exist apart and separate from the totality of a love relationship. If the relationship is guarded and sterile, the sexuality is likely to reflect that. If, in contrast, the relationship is open, adventurous, and emotionally bold, it is likely that the sexuality will be likewise. No amount of technique will address a boring sexual relationship if the emotional undercurrent is not vibrant.

Of the many forms of intimacy—a smile across the room, a shared hardship, a family ritual, a kiss, a touch—sex is probably fraught with more confusion, unrealistic expectations, misunderstanding, and disillusionment than any other. Sex promises emotional fulfillment, security, reassurance, and intimacy, even if it often fails to deliver. For both men and women, the pressure to perform sexually adds a burdensome demand to their bond. An emphasis on technique overlooks the fact that it is not about how you do it; it is about how you feel about whom you are doing it with.

Clinical exploration of sex and sexuality has vastly improved our sexual climate and washed away much ignorance and rigidity. But the concentration on sexual techniques and gimmicks, a vestige of the sexual revolution, cuts off many couples from true intimacy. Caught up in the mechanics and methods of satisfying their partner, they lose sight of the most basic aspect of sexuality: the expression of feelings. A case in point involves the experiences of Joan and Martin, both of whom have had their share of disappointing relationships.

Joan:

The man in my last relationship never expressed any appreciation for me and rarely even kissed me. It was sex and no closeness. A few months of the same unaffectionate routine contaminated our sex life. Sex became a weapon in a power struggle. If I couldn't get him to respond to me as a person, to be tender and loving, I wasn't going to respond to him physically and emotionally. I started withholding sex or giving it and going through the motions in a perfunctory manner. I was saying directly and through sex: "I want our relationship to be better—warmer, more feeling-oriented, less mechanical." That either threatened him or he misunderstood, because he became very rigid and countered with, "You're frigid; you have sexual hang-ups." That was his favorite line. In my view, our sexual problems were really relationship problems that expressed themselves sexually. I think sex enjoyment is increased by how we act toward each other in all aspects of our lives together. Sex is part of the relationship; I don't see it as a separate entity.

Martin:

I agree with Joan. I feel sex is an integral part of a relationship. That's what makes it so gratifying. When Joan and I first became physically involved, I went through a few months of fear about how good she would think my performance was and how I compared to her other lovers. I was particularly plagued by imagined comparisons to her former partner: "Was she matching our abilities as lovers? Did I measure up to him in that regard?" I also came into the situation with a backlog of negative reactions from my last relationship. Maybe in some relationships the sex stays good even if the relationship doesn't.

Not in mine. Sex became terrible, and we both traded barbs in that area. So sex with Joan—an important person in my life—was tense. I was giving myself a hard time from several quarters.

One night something interesting happened that has had a very positive effect. Joan was feeling sexier than I was, and she came on to me. I'd had a particularly grueling day and I wasn't really in the mood for sex, but she snuggled up to me and I felt compelled to respond. Things didn't go too well, though. I couldn't get aroused; I wasn't able to get an erection. So I said to Joan, "I'm sorry." She looked at me with love and tenderness and said, "Don't be sorry. You don't have to prove anything to me. I love you next to me, holding me, talking to me. You can touch me, kiss me. I love it! Our relationship is not going to be judged by erections! What I really want from you is that you are with me, that I feel the connection with you. That's what is important."

From that time on my performance fears disappeared. Joan was right. Two people who basically love each other, who express good feelings toward each other, don't need to prove through sex that they're valuable people. All they have to do is relax, be real, and enjoy each other.

While there's no ready formula for connecting sexually, being able to "relax, be real, and enjoy each other," as Martin put it, certainly helps. Some couples avoid this because they have no desire to be more intimate; they are smoldering with resentment, locked in wars of mutual withholding—in short, they like making sex unpleasant for their partner! Others are unwilling to tolerate the discomfort of moving closer, no matter what the benefits. And still others are "emotionally divorced," staying with each other only for financial and social reasons.

All this is not to suggest that there is no place for technique. We all begin our partner-related sexual experiences by focusing on technique; it is part of every adolescent and young adult's developmental tasks. The problem is that some of us never stop. We stay with the adolescent experience of sex—the how-to-do-it and performance aspect—rather than focus on our partner. The result is that we avoid contact with our partner, although we contend that we are pursuing it. Consider your own experience: would you rather have a partner who is fully with you in your lovemaking, even if he or she isn't a technical wonder, or a partner who has perfected a system of mechanical touching but does not make personal contact?

For those couples desirous of intensifying their contact during love-making, the benefits are bountiful. However, in order to do this, a couple has to go beyond the physical experience: without the intimate exchange of thoughts, feelings, and desires, even the most fiery of sexual relationships will soon dry up. Feelings of closeness and distance cannot be divorced from sexual satisfaction and dissatisfaction; a couple's relationship out of bed cannot be separated from what happens to them in bed.

In effect, sexual satisfaction often corresponds to the degree of non-sexual satisfaction within the relationship. It is unrealistic to expect that crossing the threshold into the bedroom creates a magical experience during which all the unspoken and unresolved issues of the relationship dissolve into unbridled sexual passion. It is also not realistic to expect that a boring relationship will fuel a sizzling romance.

Anger and Romance: Mutual Inhibitants

Often, what couples term "boredom" is a cover-up for long-standing but hidden resentment. The operative word here is *hidden*. Nearly every couple is going to experience flare-ups in response to an immediate situation, the occasional squabble, the slamming-door exit, or the exasperated burst of tears. Usually, squabbles and even a fiery outburst can be helpful if they bring the real issues out in the open for resolution. In other words, occasional arguments don't lead to long-term sexual turnoffs. However, the kind of anger that undermines a couple's love life is alive and well when for one reason or another it is not worked out. Here are some reasons:

- The anger is not voiced. One partner or the other harbors resentment but does not bring it to the other's attention.
- The anger is not recognized. You keep it not only from your partner but also from yourself, either by denial or minimizing ("I'm not angry, I'm just annoyed").

- The issue behind the anger is not resolved. Unresolved anger does not simply evaporate; it remains in the relationship and saps positive energy that could be directed toward romance.

Sometimes anger is intentionally used to keep intimacy at a distance. A signal that this may be occurring is when things are going along well in the relationship and suddenly one partner notices something annoying and picks a fight. Although the tension caused by the fear of intimacy is played out through anger, it is rarely recognized as such on a conscious level. Instead, it often results in sexual indifference. Harold, a forty-three-year-old man engaged to be married for the second time, used anger in anticipation of closeness. Here is what he had to say:

I was very attracted to Andrea. We both had incredibly busy weekdays with highly responsible jobs. We spent the entire weekend together, and I really looked forward to being with her—being with her sexually as well as just hanging out. But, as much as I looked forward, I always managed to pick a fight with Andrea on Friday night and screw up the weekend. I would promise myself I would not do it the next weekend, but there was always something that bothered me, and I couldn't help myself—I would lose it. Sometimes I would leave in a rage; other times I stayed but we weren't intimate sexually. Finally, I went back to therapy and figured out that I was afraid of the commitment after coming through a horrible divorce. When I worked that out, our time began to go much better. It is incredible that my fear sabotaged me that way. My anger felt very legitimate, but it was a defense. That's frightening!

Many couples genuinely want to be emotionally close to each other and share a passionate lovemaking partnership, but, as with Harold, they reach a certain point and their fears take over. One may start complaining about the other's spending, for example, or one may actually spend too much knowing full well that his or her partner will be put off. The issue splits them apart for a time, and then they become close again until they reach a point of closeness that one or the other is uncomfortable with and the pattern of sabotage repeats itself.

And then there are the children. As we have seen in previous chapters, children can easily be drawn into adult issues as a way to avoid directly expressed anger and as a way to dilute emotional closeness. The result can devastate sexual passion. Consider, for example, Evan Drake, age ten, and his mother's hovering stance with him. Ever since Evan was born, his mother, Janice Drake, has been overinvolved with him. When Evan had the slightest cough, merely a hint of a cough in fact, she ran to the pediatrician immediately. If Evan fell when he was learning to walk, she was there before he even hit the carpet. When Evan became frustrated during play, his mother was on the scene to remove the obstacle instantly. Janice Drake was the only mother to remain in school on Evan's first day of kindergarten, despite reassurances from his teacher and the school counselor. After all, Evan has no health problems, nor does he have special emotional or educational needs.

A typical scene in the Drake household: after overhearing his wife convincing Evan that he shouldn't go out for a bike ride because it rained the day before and the ground may still be wet, Mr. Drake was furious. Mrs. Drake attempted to talk to her husband about what had just happened, but he was so angry with her that he locked himself in his garage workshop to avoid his wife. Inside the garage he muttered, "Not only is she ruining that boy, she is more attentive to his every breath than she is to me! It's no wonder I have no interest in making love to her."

Mrs. Drake's overfunctioning with her son reflects an apparent imbalance in the family relationship. If Evan itches, Mrs. Drake scratches. In response, Mr. Drake has withdrawn from both his son and his wife. The enmeshed closeness between Mrs. Drake and her son makes it difficult to achieve a sense of closeness between she and her husband.

Frequently in a relationship that is imbalanced there is a void that both marital partners are not addressing. The destructive pattern may have evolved to fill the marital void or it may be the result of a void. Voids are created as a result of several factors, including a parent who overworks, leaving the other parent inclined toward overinvolvement with the children; a parent who is excessively fearful regarding the well-being of a child; and a parent who is lonely and directs too much energy toward a child.

Whether the pattern is cause or effect may not be the critical factor. The essential factor is the acknowledgment of the problem and collaborative resolution. In the case of the Drakes, for example, Mrs. Drake feels that her husband buries himself in his interests and neglects her. Mr. Drake counters that he doesn't "bury" himself so much as distract himself because his wife is so involved in their son. Neither concedes, and each accuses the other of being neglectful of the relationship. Both Mr. and Mrs. Drake are angry, and their sex life, which is practically nonexistent, is paying the price.

Often, the origin of child-based issues that create anger and serve as an obstacle to sexual passion dates back to a couple's own childhood. Mr. and Mrs. Jensen sought therapy because they were very concerned about their twelve-year-old son, Kenneth. Kenneth had behavior problems at school, and he was often in conflict with his father as well. Mrs. Jensen did not take the family problem lightly. She was literally losing sleep over it. As she put it, "Kenneth isn't really a bad kid; he's just not as obedient as his father insists he should be. I've tried as much as possible to step in between Kenneth and his father and to work out the problems, but my efforts only have a temporary effect. Things settle down for a few days and then they erupt all over again, as if I never said a word. I am afraid this will tear all of us apart. I am beside myself with worry, and my husband is very angry with me for interfering. He has withdrawn emotionally and sexually."

To find out how Mrs. Jensen's family of origin was influencing her relationship with her husband and son, she was asked to describe how her family functioned during her growing-up years. She characterized her father as a harsh, bitter man who reacted very strongly to anything or anyone that crossed him. Her brother was the family scapegoat, and he played his role well. He had more than his share of trouble in school and in the community, having been arrested twice for delinquent offenses. Mrs. Jensen's mother was the rescuer. On many occasions she "saved" her son from her husband's wrath by keeping untoward incidents from her husband. As a child, Mrs. Jensen had many times witnessed instances during which her mother stepped in and "protected" her brother and herself from her father's temper.

Mr. Jensen described his family as strongly patriarchal. His father, as he put it, was "king" of the house, requiring blind and immediate obedience. His mother was a quiet woman who deferred to her husband on everyday matters as well as on more important decisions. As a young child, Mr. Jensen began taking responsibility for chores and catering to the needs of his parents. Any infractions of his father's strict household rules were met with swift and strong punishment.

Mr. Jensen considered himself a "real" man and viewed the typical American upbringing as outrageously permissive. He felt that his wife was bringing up their children in a manner that was a disservice to them. "How are they going to make it in the real world?" was one of his most-used phrases. He felt that his father, who died while he was still young, had done his best to prepare him for the realities of life. The blueprint that his father had created for him contained the elements of hard work, obedience, and punishment for breaking the rules. And Mr. Jensen had assumed his role well. He demanded from his children exactly what his father had expected of him, and he used similar tactics of fear and force.

It is also apparent that Mrs. Jensen had assumed the role of rescuer in her family with Mr. Jensen, much as her own mother had done with her brother. With such opposing families of origin, it is not all that surprising that Mr. and Mrs. Jensen were at odds with each other and sexually distant.

All parents disagree, at least some of the time. Disagreement itself is not necessarily bad, nor does it have to lead to unresolved anger. For example, a variation on the drama that unfolded in the Jensen household may have gone quite differently. Mrs. Jensen could have waited until Kenneth went to sleep or quietly called her husband aside for a "parental meeting" rather than intervening between Kenneth and his father.

Mr. Jensen could also have approached the situation with his son differently. Considering that his relationship with Kenneth was very strained and their interaction formed a negative, repetitive pattern, he could have talked with his wife before approaching his son. Even if Mr. Jensen and Mrs. Jensen failed to reach a consensus, they would have at least had the opportunity to discuss their differences and develop problem-solving options. This type of give and take is vital for the development of a successful marriage and a vibrant sexual relationship.

Intimacy Fears in the Bedroom

Although sex is only one link in the chain of relating intimately, it is, to most of us, invested with a great deal of importance. We all hunger for the passion that was present in the early part of our love relationship. In fact, if couples don't experience a deep level of lovemaking, it is usually because one or both are afraid of becoming truly intimate with each other. They are together, but they know how to connect only through the genitals. Without realizing it, they are stuck at the level of hormonally driven sex, and when the wake of roiling hormones has subsided, sexual passion fades.

Women, in particular, often complain about men's failure or inability to be intimate with them. What they mean is that he doesn't listen; he doesn't talk about his feelings. Men often assume that intimacy is what happens when you have sex with someone, and they don't understand why women fail to recognize what an intimate act lovemaking is. "Why do I have to talk about my feelings when I'm showing them?" they may ask. Here's what Lauren, age forty-nine, said:

> When Matt and I got married twenty-five years ago, we lived in the hot zone. Passion was everything to us. We sustained a high level of pure physical passion longer than our other married friends did, but gradually things began to change for us too. He had the first affair, and then I had one. The excitement generated by the affairs—the tearful confessions, the angry recriminations, the dramatic reunions— made our relationship hot again, but we couldn't sustain the heat.
>
> Eventually he did the predictable thing. He left me when I was forty for a woman half his age. Exhausted from being the drama queen, I went into therapy, where I learned we could probably have saved our marriage and our sex life if we'd been vulnerable and open to each other. But we didn't, and I've moved on. My second marriage is different, better. We are more connected to each other on all levels

than Matt and I ever were. At almost fifty I'm having the best sex I've ever had—and, in my case, that's saying a lot. This time the sex is deeply emotional.

Lauren reports that sex is better now, the second time around, in a marriage with a man who shares more than his genitals. What does that tell you about the erotic power of openness? Being open with a long-time partner should be easy, but it isn't for many people. Years of squelching their anger, denying their guilt, and suppressing their emotions have left many couples afraid of being honest. To be honest is to be vulnerable. What if your feelings are rejected? What if your partner harshly judges and withdraws? Emotionally disrobing in front of another person is more frightening than physically disrobing, yet it is more necessary for great sex. That kind of intimacy will seem less fearful to you if you follow these suggestions:

- Stop taking your partner's behavior personally. A partner's tension, anger, sadness, need for privacy, or moods may have nothing to do with you, and you aren't responsible for solving all the problems, or for your partner's feelings.

- Challenge your own negative thoughts that inhibit sexuality. You may be angry about something that happened at work or unhappy with your body following a weight gain. Those negative thoughts are likely to make you too angry or uptight to be loving. Work at developing an optimistic attitude toward your life. Optimism is a hopeful view of the future. Optimism gives us more than solace when times aren't good; it plays a role in reducing anxiety, alleviating the emotional distress accompanying many life events, and motivating us toward achieving personal and professional goals.

- Use your vulnerability to be a better lover. If you work at becoming more comfortable with your vulnerability, you will be more understanding of, and comfortable with, a partner's insecurity and doubt. *Expose* rather than *protect* yourself emotionally. This openness will allow you to touch your partner in a more intimate way.

- Let go of the need to control your partner. Before you can take charge of your own sexuality, you have to stop trying to control your partner. Few of us are ever really successful at controlling our partner's behavior sexually or otherwise, though we expend a lot of energy in trying. Maybe you think your sex life would improve if your partner took the initiative more often or were more willing to try different positions or would make love at the times you would prefer or would wear high heels to bed or would bring home flowers more often. Let it go. Work on yourself. In growing and changing, you will more likely excite your partner than if you pressure him or her to conform to your vision. The more you become a complete person—as opposed to half a couple—the less you will feel the need to control your partner. What's more, contrary to what you might fear, focusing on yourself doesn't give your partner license to do nothing. In fact, when you stop focusing on your partner and start clarifying what you want and what you need to do to get it, you are setting a very powerful example.

- Be open about your sexual preferences and desires. Many of us have been brought up to be sexually shy and inhibited. During lovemaking it is not uncommon for a couple to be reluctant to communicate with each other, directly or indirectly, for a variety of reasons: embarrassment, fear, or self-consciousness ("I don't want to admit that I like those things; I want them to just happen"). For better or worse, these kinds of things seldom "just happen." Each individual's source of stimulation is a highly personal and variable matter; maintaining a wall of silence around sexual feelings forces partners to make assumptions that may be incorrect—or correct one time and incorrect another. In effect, expressing sexual preferences and desires is another way of being more fully known by your partner; it is a particularly sensitive aspect of being open with each other that many couples, even those with considerable sexual experience, may find difficult.

Joyce and Peter are one such couple. Joyce had lived with a man for two years and had had a number of brief affairs prior to meeting Peter. Peter had been married for five years and had dated extensively after his divorce. When he met Joyce he had been single for three years and felt ready for another try at a committed relationship. Six months of dating convinced both Joyce and Peter to tie the knot. Besides their sexual attraction, they shared similar hopes and dreams and felt very much in love.

After two years of marriage, Joyce's sexual interest began to gradually wane. Peter, disappointed, hurt, and confused, blamed marriage. "We never had any problem with sex before we married," he complained. When Joyce defended their decision to marry, Peter retorted by accusing her of faking sexual interest in order to "hook" him. The underlying difficulty was not the decision to marry, nor was it any pretense on Joyce's part to be sexually interested. In fact, she was quite disturbed by her diminishing sexual satisfaction with Peter.

Joyce and Peter's initial lovemaking had been inflamed by passion; the excitement of discovery, of novelty, had promised to spring their fantasies to life. It had been a glorious time when the hours sped by and the nights were never long enough. But this early sexual excitement soon cooled down, as often occurs. Actually, Peter was as caught up in the "cooling down" as Joyce was. Their lovemaking had become routine.

Invariably Peter would indicate that he felt like having sex. Joyce would agree because she felt she should. Because Joyce was not as eager as she had been in the early days of their relationship, she was slower in becoming aroused—lubrication was insufficient—and Peter found entry difficult, while Joyce experienced discomfort. Peter remained silent about his lack of enjoyment; Joyce passively endured her displeasure. Complaints were occasionally exchanged ("If I didn't come on to you, we'd never have sex"; "I have other things on my mind;

all you ever think about is sex!"), but the substance of their complaints remained untouched.

Joyce and Peter's plight is one that frequently occurs in an ongoing relationship. As their sexual relationship became less stimulating, they had increased difficulty talking about it and, consequently, became demoralized and resentful. In contrast, if openness had replaced secretiveness, if experimentation and sexual variety had replaced rigidity and stagnation, pleasure would have likely returned to their relationship and reinforced their enthusiasm for lovemaking.

- Master the art of surrender. Surrender is the opposite of control. In the context of erotica, "surrender" is often used when the heroine allows herself to be swept away by the hero's passion. That's a very narrow view of erotic surrender. It limits the woman and leaves out the man entirely. Think of erotic surrender as the act of letting go while aroused, not as ceding control to your partner. Most people enjoy the feeling of being in control of their lives, even though much of what happens to them is clearly beyond their control. Successful people are admired not only for the money they earn and their accomplishments but also for the amount of control they exert over their environment and the others inside it. People who practice self-discipline are also admired. In lovemaking, the man who can "control" his erection and ejaculation and the woman who can "control" her partner's arousal and her own responses are idealized. Where does surrender fit into this picture?

Surrender is an integral part of true intimacy. Letting go into full arousal is intrinsic to the higher level of sexual pleasures. It takes time to become comfortable with the process. Surrender is no easy matter. It's frightening to keep thinking, "I can't let go completely," but it makes sense to be frightened if you believe that you will lose yourself and not find your way back. Letting go requires a strong grip on yourself. It is about knowing who you are and being willing to reveal that and stand by it. In effect, it is a paradox: you will be able to let go when you have a good grip on yourself and who you are. It is akin to climbing a mountain. If you feel in control of yourself, rather than directing your energy trying to control the elements—the terrain and the weather—you can relax and take in the beauty of the climb. When you're tense and feeling out of control, the climb seems foreboding.

Are you receptive to sexual surrender? Here are some suggestions to begin: (1) Turn yourself over to your partner. Offer to be your partner's sexual slave for a night. He or she can create a sexual script within reason. You may discover a new dimension to your sexuality this way. (2) Write a short essay on "Why I don't let go sexually." State all your reasons. Then describe how your life might change if you surrendered to your sexuality. Elaborate. Don't merely say, for example, "I would be embarrassed." What is the basis of the embarrassment? How would the embarrassment feel? How would you and your partner handle it? Put your essay aside for a few days. Read it again and write a rebuttal. (3) Play a role opposite the one you typically play in bed for one week. If you are passive, become active. Initiate lovemaking. Be bold and assertive in getting your needs met. If you are active, be passive in all aspects of lovemaking. Don't be afraid of the new feelings these changes will generate. Give in to them.

Turning Up the Emotional Heat

If you have more successfully confronted anger, fear of intimacy, and an overemphasis on performance in your sexual relationship, you are ready to turn up the emotional heat by using eye contact. Eye contact can be very powerful—and it is very telling. Consider some circumstances where eye contact, or lack of it, may convey something about what is going on: Recall, for instance, your family dinners when you were a kid. Were faces uplifted and animated, or did everyone stare awkwardly at their plate? Was eye contact natural and comforting? Or was eye contact avoided at all costs, especially in relation to some family members? What did the eye contact (or avoidance) signify?

Then there is the simple experience of walking down the street. Eyes meet, people realize they're making contact, and sometimes it feels good—and other times it may not. This is especially true if one feels "undressed" or violated by the person looking at him or her and is offended, even though nothing physical actually happened. Standing near someone in an elevator, most of us watch the floor numbers light up rather than make eye contact. Eye contact in a confined space with a stranger feels too intimate. In other circumstances, the impact may be different; some of us, for example, have experienced the sizzle of "electric" eye contact with a stranger across the room.

Considering the power of eye contact, it is striking that sex in the dark with eyes closed is so common. On the other hand, it is quite understandable. Many of us have to "tune out" to get close enough to make love; we don't want to be distracted from our fantasies of being with someone else!

One couple discovered eye contact in their lovemaking and found it to have a profound effect. "Jerry and I read some books on Tantric sex to liven things up," Lisa said. She and Jerry, both divorced and in their early forties, have been in a monogamous relationship for ten years, though they don't live together. She continued:

The best ideas were the simple ones, especially keeping your eyes open during lovemaking. I'd gotten in the habit of using fantasies during lovemaking, and I thought I wouldn't be able to climax without them. So I closed my eyes and had my own fantasies; I was having sex almost alone. Once I began keeping my eyes open, I didn't need the fantasies as often. I began really paying attention to Jerry, feeling and experiencing him in a new way, as well as experiencing my own arousal on a deeper level. It made familiar behaviors seem like new things we'd never done.

The eye lock, looking deeply into one another's eyes and holding the gaze, is the most intensely intimate experience either one of us has ever had. Initially, just thinking about it made me self-conscious, and it intimidated me. But I talked myself out of avoiding it. "What's so bad about being self-conscious? It is an aspect of growth, letting my lover see more of me," is what I reminded myself. And I'm so glad I did! The first time I looked into his eyes at the point of orgasm, I was blown away by the emotions I felt. The orgasm was so much more complex. He had the same experience. Truthfully, it took some time before I had the courage to do it. I never realized how hard it is to let someone you love get that close to you! Opening your eyes is the best way to connect more strongly with your partner. Every time it happens it brings to mind how far our relationship and our love have come. I don't know why it took us ten years to discover, but I'm thrilled that we have. Our lovemaking is so much more exciting.

Studies have shown that 90 percent of women close their eyes while kissing. Only a third of men do. During orgasm, men are still more likely to keep their eyes open than women, but the majority of both genders either close their eyes or look away from their partner at the moment of climax. Men often bury their faces in a woman's neck or a pillow. There are several reasons for this behavior. Some people may fear that open eyes will disconnect them from their own sensations. In contrast, others may feel emotionally distant from their partners and wish to avoid anything that will intensify their experience. Body-image issues may force some, especially women, into hiding behind their own eyelids. Or they may feel awkward about exposing themselves this way. To feel comfortable looking your partner in the eyes, you'll have to confront conflicts and issues you've swept under the rug, which is why some couples continue to make love with eyes closed. We are never so vulnerable as when we allow our sexual arousal to be seen. You aren't likely to let your partner look deep inside you until you've done that yourself. As noted earlier, if you're avoiding your partner (or yourself) when you're not in bed, you're not likely to act differently between the sheets.

Rather than diminishing erotic pleasure, keeping your eyes open during lovemaking turns up the emotional heat. Some Tantric sexual positions utilize this concept to help lovers transcend routine lovemaking and achieve a deeper, more spiritual union—as does the Kaballah, a book of Jewish mysticism. Meaningful eye contact during lovemaking intensifies the physical sensations by deepening the emotional connection between lovers. Here are some suggestions for more eye-opening lovemaking:

- Open your eyes occasionally while kissing. The visual stimulation will probably increase your arousal as well as provide your partner useful feedback on how you are feeling about the kiss. Some studies have suggested that men bond more intensely with women when they make eye contact during kissing.

- Practice the eye lock. Look deeply into each other's eyes as you are caressing each other. Hold the look. Do this more than once. You probably won't realize how little you look into each other's eyes during lovemaking until you practice the eye lock.

- Make frequent eye contact during oral sex. Glance up from your partner's genitals while performing oral sex. Make eye contact. The impact can be electrifying.

- Look into each other's eyes during intercourse. The face-to-face intercourse positions encourage eye contact. Utilize the opportunities inherent in those positions. Don't look away when you feel arousal increase or when the connection intensifies your feelings.

- Open your eyes during orgasm. Eyes-open orgasms may feel more explosive and emotional than other orgasms; the afterglow may be more tender and prolonged. Looking into your lover's eyes at the moment of orgasm is like an erotic gift. Even if the concentration isn't always intense, the practice is likely to generate greater feelings of closeness.

Afterplay

After having an intimate and passionate lovemaking experience, don't leave! There's dessert, in the form of "afterplay." Afterplay describes whatever a couple does immediately following lovemaking, most often cuddling, caressing, and sharing intimate thoughts. This experience, described in my book *Secrets of Better Sex*, may last no more than a few minutes before the partners go to sleep or get out of bed, but it is important to both men and women. People are more vulnerable to each other after sex than they are at other times. Tender and affectionate afterplay is one of the keys to improving a sexual relationship.

When a couple has experienced difficulty during sex, they often feel uneasy with each other afterward. Embarrassed or afraid to talk about what happened, or didn't happen, they pull away from each other, both physically and emotionally. Other couples may use the time after good sex to ask favors of each other or work out a nonsexual issue between them. Afraid of postcoital vulnerability, some men—and some women, too—turn on the television or get up and fix something to eat or roll over and go to sleep immediately after orgasm. They are wasting a good opportunity to enhance the intimate bond.

"I know mine is the familiar wifely complaint," Nancy said. "After sex, my husband jumps out of bed, cleans himself, and then either comes back to bed and falls right to sleep or turns on the television and gets absorbed in Leno or Letterman. On Saturday night, he offers to fix us a snack. The sex is good, but I want a little cuddling afterward. I want him to hold me and say tender things. Why can't he do that?"

Nancy's husband, Joe, was also satisfied with their sex life. His only complaint about her was that she didn't understand his need for space afterward. "Nancy feels like I'm rejecting her in some way, but I'm not," he insisted.

When Joe understood how important afterplay was to Nancy, they reached a compromise. When he came back to bed after using the bathroom, he promised he wouldn't turn on the TV or fall asleep for at least ten minutes. During that time he would hold her; she in turn promised that she wouldn't use those intimate moments to say things he didn't want to hear, such as reminding him he wasn't doing his share of the household chores. To his surprise, he liked the cuddling. Afterplay has become important to him as well. Joe and Nancy have also learned more about each other's sexual desires and preferences by exchanging confidences as they lie contented in each other's arms. They are now incorporating some of these desires into their lovemaking—desires that would have remained unexpressed if they hadn't grown closer to each other during afterplay.

There may be times, of course, when two people who care deeply for each other want nothing more than to roll to their opposite sides and sleep. Nearly everyone reaches a point in an intimate relationship when they just need to be alone for a while. And not every sexual encounter should play out the same way afterward. Afterplay should not become another way to measure performance.

Some suggestions for sexy afterplay: don't use afterplay as a sexual postmortem. If something about the lovemaking does need to be discussed, do so at another time. Afterplay is not a platform for airing sexual grievances. Do express sexual feelings and thoughts you've not shared. Afterplay is a good time to share what you enjoy about the sexual interaction but feel too shy to point out during sex. Don't bring problems into afterplay. It is not the time to discuss the checkbook. Nonverbal interaction such as cuddling strengthens closeness, as do the words, "I love you," which have a special meaning in these tender moments.

AFTERWORD

When I completed the last chapter, I felt finished. After all, I fleshed out the issue of openness in love relationships in just the manner I had proposed to my editor. I even scanned other books that have addressed some of the issues herein, and I liked the perspective that I brought to the subject better. I sat back with satisfaction. Then, one day, several weeks later, I was riffling through the *New York Times Book Review*. Something caught my eye and grabbed my attention. It was a work of fiction, a fascinating account of openness between a man and a woman.

Here's the story: a married man spots a woman, who is also married, at a party. He writes her a letter proposing an affair. It is not to be the usual affair in that they will never meet, nor have any contact outside of correspondence. They will not even hear each other's voices, because, as the man states in his letter, "Even a voice is too real for the hallucination I want to have with you." Their written contact will also be quite out of the norm. The relationship he is suggesting is one that will be fully and uninhibitedly open. His letter suggests that, "We could be like two people who inject themselves with truth serum and at long last have to tell it, the truth. I want to be able to say to myself, 'I bled truth with her,' yes, that's what I want. Be a knife for me, and I, I swear, will be a knife for you."

I haven't read the book, just the review. However, as unusual as it seems, it occurs to me that it would be extraordinary if the man had proposed the "truth serum" approach to his wife. Now there's an idea that sounds very exciting, and terrifying. I suspect that many of us have, somewhere in our psyche, the hunger to be fully known and accepted—even those, especially those, who hold up their hand in protest. The secret wish we have is to have one more chance to be like that small child who puts it all out there without self-consciousness; to have nothing significant to defend, no secrets to hide, no tension about "being found out." It would be wonderful to feel secure enough to be able to shout, "This is who I am, and I can embrace all of me!"

This desire is probably a hidden basis for going into psychotherapy for many people. The obvious reason is to deal with a presenting problem. The less obvious reason is to be known, to oneself and to another. Of course, seeing a psychologist is relatively safe. It is like the affair proposed in the book review. The disclosures occur between two people (although in the case of psychotherapy it is mostly one-way) whose lives do not intersect outside of a limited context.

To even the most casual observer of couples, it is apparent that the kind of experience that occurs in the affair described is not one that most married people have with each other, not even close. We've all heard of the man or woman who "spills his (her) guts" to an anonymous stranger on a plane or in some other situation where the contact is temporary and the listener is not part of his or her day-to-day life. And that is the point: after giving the other person a glimpse into your soul, you don't have to see him or her or worry about some lasting judgment he or she has made. In the fantasy account, the man is taking special precautions to make the experience as impersonal as possible while he shares the most personal aspects of himself.

Loving without reservation, letting another person—someone whom you have to face the next day and every day—view you emotionally naked, takes a degree of faith, self-awareness, and, perhaps more than anything, courage. It is the courage to believe in yourself enough to be revealing and to tolerate how naked and unsettled the intensity of the experience leaves you feeling. It requires that you accept yourself and your humanness—including shortcomings—and accept that with your imperfections you are still worthwhile. You have to take responsibility for your feelings and regard yourself enough to express them. It is a refusal to tolerate your own self-deceptions and to face your deepest truths. Doing this with your love partner is like walking a razor's edge. It is not for the faint of heart, and it doesn't make life easier or painless. It just makes life sweeter and the pain more meaningful.

Do you dare to look into yourself and without reservation share what you find with the person you sleep with regularly? Are you willing to face yourself and your lover each day? Like anything that is worthwhile, it is not without risks. Nowhere is more gained or lost or more energy squandered—nowhere are more lessons learned—than in love relationships. And nothing teaches us so much about others and ourselves as living authentically with another person.

BIBLIOGRAPHY

Bach, George. *The Intimate Enemy*. New York: William Morrow, Inc., 1968.

Block, Joel D. *Broken Promises, Mended Hearts: Maintaining Trust in Love Relationships*. Chicago: Contemporary Books, 2001.

———. *Friendship*. New York: Macmillan Publishing Co., Inc., 1980.

———. *Secrets of Better Sex*. New York: Parker Publishing Co., 1996.

Block, Joel D., and Susan S. Bartell. *Mommy or Daddy, Whose Side Am I On?* Boston: Adams Media, 2002.

Erikson, Erik. *Childhood and Society*. New York: W. W. Norton, 1950.

Fast, Julius, and Barbara Fast. *Talking Between the Lines*. New York: Viking Press, 1979.

Gordon, Neil. Review of *Be My Knife*, by David Grossman. *New York Times Book Review*, 13 January 2002, 7.

Gottman, John. *Why Marriages Succeed or Fail*. New York: Simon and Schuster, 1994.

Harlow, Harry F., and M. Harlow. "The Nature of Love," *American Psychologist* 13 (1958): 673–85.

Hawthorne, Nathaniel. *The Scarlet Letter*. New York: Washington Square Press, 1955.

Kazan, Elia. *The Arrangement.* New York: Stein & Day, 1967.

Lague, Louise. "How Honest Are Couples, Really?" *Reader's Digest*, August 2001, 88–99.

Levenson, Robert, L. L. Carstensen, and John Gottman. "The Influence of Age and Gender on Affect, Physiology, and Their Interrelations: A Study of Long-Term Marriages." *Journal of Personality and Social Psychology* 67 (1994): 56–68.

Lorenz, Konrad. *On Aggression.* New York: Harcourt Brace & World, Inc., 1966.

Rilke, Rainer Maria. *Ahead of the Parting: The Selected Poetry and Prose of Rainer Maria Rilke.* New York: Modern Library, 1995.

Roth, Henry. *Call It Sleep.* New York: Cooper Square Publishers, Inc., 1934.

Watzlawick, Paul, John Weakland, and Paul Fisch. *Change.* New York: Norton, 1974.

INDEX